SURRENDER AT DACCA
BIRTH OF A NATION

SURRENDER AT DACCA

Birth of a Nation

LT GEN J F R JACOB

MANOHAR
1997

First published 1997

© Lt Gen J F R Jacob, 1997

ISBN 81-7304-189-X

Published by
Ajay Kumar Jain for
Manohar Publishers & Distributors
2/6 Ansari Road, Daryaganj
New Delhi 110 002

Typeset by
A J Software Publishing Co. Pvt. Ltd.
305 Durga Chambers, 1333 D B Gupta Road
Karol Bagh, New Delhi 110 005

Printed at
Replika Press Pvt Ltd
A-229, DSIDC Narela Industrial Park
Delhi 110 040

To
The Indian Army
and
The Regiment of Artillery

I've eaten your bread and your salt.
I've drunk your water and wine.
The deaths ye died I've watched beside
and the lives ye lived were mine.

RUDYARD KIPLING

Contents

LIST OF ILLSUTRATIONS

Between pages   40-1

1. Jack Jacob as an Officer Cadet in 1942
2. No. 1 Platoon 'A' Company Officers' Training School
   Mhow, 1942. Jack Jacob top row fifth from left, to his
   right 'Tappy' Raina

Preface

The swift decisive offensive launched by the Indian Army on 4 December 1971, culminating in the surrender of the Pakistani Eastern Command within a mere thirteen days is surely the greatest military feat in our history. Some twenty-five years have since elapsed but so far no authoritative or objective account is available. An official history has been prepared but is yet to be published; in any case its authors were not given access to sensitive documents. Their work will, as is the current practice, be subjected to editing by the Defence, Home and External Affairs Ministries, and will by and large conform to the official version of events. Since the Henderson Brooks Report on the 1962 operations and the history of the 1965 operations have yet to be published, it is more than likely that the account of the 1971 campaign will not see the light of day for quite some time yet.

I was appointed Chief of Staff of Eastern Command in May 1969, an appointment I held until June 1972. This was a period which saw the growing involvement of the Army with the events in the region and proved to be a critical time for us. The Naxalite insurgency in West Bengal had reached such proportions that it became doubtful if the Assembly Elections due soon, would be held. We had to deploy two Army divisions and 50 Parachute Brigade so that a stable environment could be created and the elections held. Soon after, the crack-down of the Pakistani Army on the people of East Pakistan, now Bangladesh, created a situation such that our troops had to be retained in West Bengal to meet the contingencies arising out of the instability in East Pakistan. We, at Command Headquarters, realised that hostilities could break out any time between India and Pakistan and that war was inevitable. However, it was not the outcome of the war that worried us, confident as we were of victory; it was the political ramifications that proved more intractable. As it turned out, the advantages gained on the battlefield were frittered away in the political negotiations at Simla in 1972. The creation of Bangladesh had an impact on the geopolitical environment that had not quite been foreseen and certainly not adequately prepared for.

The waging of war is a complex business involving almost all sections of the population. The conduct and progress of military operations is far from smooth and never wholly predictable. The successful planning and conduct of operations depends on imaginative planning, flexibility of approach, the capacity to react, and foresight so as not to be overtaken by events. Moreover, military operations require sound infrastructural and logistic backing. Luck too plays an important part. Therefore, it is important to study the political and military background of the operations we have been engaged in to draw the relevant lessons—political, military and infrastructural. It is with this is mind that I have set out to write an account of the 1971 war and the build-up to the military operations in the Eastern Theatre—an event with which I was closely associated and of which I have first-hand knowledge.

After the 1971 war, India emerged as a regional superpower. Her geostrategic interests encompass not only the Indian Ocean but areas adjacent to and beyond its land frontiers. A future war, if and when it does come, will be of a longer duration than the conflicts of 1965 and 1971. The pattern of operations too is likely to be different. Infrastuctural and industrial complexes are almost certain to

10

be targeted. It is, therefore, all the more necessary that we learn from past mistakes so that we are better prepared to face the future. I hope this work will go some way towards fulfilling that object.

In 1962, 1965 and even in 1971 we lacked a comprehensive geostrategic and geomilitary assessment of our interests and the threats to these interests. There were no clear-cut political aims or directives. There was no effective machinery to plan, coordinate and execute war, and even today we lack a permanent Chief of the Defence Staff or an adequately staffed support organization. There is no National Security Council and even if one materializes in the near future, it is likely to be, like its short-lived predecessor, superficial and toothless. Intelligence acquisition, and more importantly assessments, have in the past been far short of the minimum operational levels required. There appears to be no appreciable improvement in this regard to this day. I have, therefore, endeavoured to draw lessons from the build up and operations culminating in the liberation of Bangladesh so that we can learn to draw the right conclusions and apply them, suitably updated and modified, to meet the new emerging challenges ahead. I recall a former Prime Minister remarking that he did not need to study history as he made history. But it is also a truism that those who do not learn from history are destined to repeat it. I, for one, have learnt a great deal from the study of military history. I trust that this book will contribute towards an understanding of the problems of planning a campaign from its very inception to the building up of the required infrastructure, logistics and finally, the conduct and control of operations.

New Delhi, 1997   J F R Jacob

Early Years

It was 31 July 1978. My four-year tenure as Army Commander had come to an end. I was putting on my uniform for the last time. I buckled on my Sam Browne and inserted the sheathed sword into the frog. The leather shone with a brilliance that only a Gorkha batman with traditional spit polish and elbow grease could achieve! I looked at myself in the mirror: the peaked cap had its customary tilt to the right, a tilt that in the old days many a well-intentioned senior had tried unsuccessfully to rectify. I was ready to leave for my last day at Headquarters, Eastern Command in Fort William. Officers and men waited, some apprehensive about my successor who was to arrive the next day. I passed through the various offices saying my final good-byes.

A ceremonial guard of honour was drawn up in front of the gun park. Fascinated by the varieties of cannons I had encountered during my travels, I had acquired some rare pieces and had them installed as a monument to the Eastern Army. The bronze and brass cannons collected here represented many a stream of Indian history—a cannon cast for Emperor Aurangzeb, still bearing the imprint of hits of cannon ball; a cannon from the Army of Maharaja Ranjit Singh; one cast in Fort William; another from a Dutch ship and a cannon from the Battle of Plassey.

Dark monsoon clouds drifted slowly past, the sun trying to pierce their opacity. Occasional shafts of sunlight accentuated polished brass and shining boots. There were familiar faces in the guard of honour, many of whom had mounted guard at my residence. I drove out with the pilot and outriders, past lines of soldiers giving the traditional Army send off with cries of 'General Jacob Sahib Ki Jai', past the officers' mess fronted with two granite lions, one alert and one couchant. I had moved these lions from Princep Ghat, a landing stage on the river Hoogly, when it was being demolished for the construction of a controversial bridge. The motorcade then moved out of the Fort through the main sortie of East Gate, formerly named Plassey Gate, into the city of Calcutta.

It seemed only fitting that an Army career that began with my passing through Plassey Gate in the early summer of 1941, should end with a ceremonial drive through this same gate. Memories flashed back to that hot, bright April day. The black asphalt road was shimmering in the heat haze as with trepidation I cycled through Plassey Gate and over the moat. The sentry from the British Garrison Battalion stopped me as I approached. He wore stiffly starched khaki shorts, hosetops, anklets, highly polished boots and a solar topee—compulsory headgear in those days. When informed that I had been called for an interview for a commission, the sentry directed me to the Area Headquarters. I cycled past the huge four-storied barracks that housed a complete battalion, its offices, stores and ancillaries, possibly the largest single barrack on this planet.

The Area Commander, Maj Gen Heydeman interviewed me. My first impression of him was that of a stern and unsmiling man, but as the interview progressed the stiff mask began to soften. We talked of school and college, cricket, rugger and my tenure in the Cadet Corps. After a long chat he told me that I would be called for another interview at General Headquarters at Simla. I cycled out of the For through Plassey Gate with a light heart: a new life was about to begin!

Simla, then the summer capital of British India, is a salubrious Himalayan hill station nestling on wooded coniferous ridges. The Government of India and General Headquarters would shift, every summer, from the heat and dust of Delhi to the cool of the hills. The buildings that housed the Army Headquarters were unique, wood on a steel frame whose joints were engineered to absorb earthquake shocks. Large monkeys swung and gambolled along the corridors, snarling and snapping at anyone foolhardy enough to try and chase them away.

The interview was conducted by a board of officers clad in gaberdine service dress, assisted by a lesser Maharaja. Questions revolved around social background, school, university, games, *shikar* and current affairs. The war, a thousand miles away, seemed many thousands further. I was told to await further instructions from the Officers Training School.

In October 1941 I arrived at the Officers Training School at Mhow. Mhow was a British Cantonment established in the early part of the nineteenth century. The name Mhow is believed to be an acronym for 'Military Headquarters of War'. It is more likely a corruption of the name of the village of Mau, in close proximity to the Cantonment. The Cantonment assumed importance during the Mutiny of the Bengal Army in 1857. Of the three East India Company Armies, the Madras, Bombay and Bengal, only the Bengal Army had mutinied, and it was at Mhow that Gen Sir Hugh Rose had concentrated elements of the Bombay Army to move against the Rani of Jhansi.

Life as a cadet was hard. Training was tough but we were treated as officers. We were lodged two to a room and were allotted a bearer to help us with domestic chores and to polish boots and belts. The course was to be of six months duration. However, in February 1942 I was called to the Company Commander's office and asked to volunteer for the Artillery. I replied that I had not given the Artillery as my first choice and as my performance so far had been good I should get my choice of combat arm. He replied that I was to do exactly as I was told and ended the interview. The Artillery then was not a popular choice as it meant an extra period of training, resulting in being commissioned some months later than the other cadets. Further, the Artillery School at Deolali, after it was moved from Kakul, was in those early days poorly housed with few basic amenities and had a reputation for failing to qualify a high proportion of its intake.

I was given a few days leave and then asked to proceed to Deolali. It was the summer of 1942. We were housed four to a tent. We had to study at night by the light of a hurricane lamp. The staff were inexperienced if not incompetent. Our instructor was a reserve officer, a 'box wallah' (a business man) from a jute company in Calcutta. His assistant was a bombardier from a regular field regiment with no teaching qualifications, who spent more time berating us instead of teaching us methodically. Even so, it was seven weeks of the most concentrated training I have ever had. We were trained on a variety of equipment: obsolete 18 pounder guns, 4.5 inch howitzers and later that dependable gun, the 25 pounder. Two-thirds of the cadets on the course managed to qualify; the remainder were sent back to the Infantry. I left Deolali on 7 June 1942 with a shiny pip on each shoulder, a Second Lieutenant.

After a short spell at the training division in August 1942 I was sent on an assignment to a regiment in the middle-east. The voyage from Bombay to Basra was uneventful. We officers were comfortably housed in cabins and dined in congenial surroundings, but life for the rank and file was far from comfortable—open decks, inadequate toilet facilities and badly-cooked food. Most of the soldiers were seasick and the stench from the decks was nauseating. It was with great relief that we sailed up the tranquil waters of the Shatt el-Arab, past the refinery at Abadan to anchor at the date palm-lined port of Basra. I spent a few days in the transit camp at Shaiba before proceeding by goods train to Baghdad. I must have contracted sand fly fever at Shaiba and on arrival at Baghdad was admitted to the British Military Hospital, which was housed in one of the palaces on the outskirts of Baghdad.

Soon after I recovered, I was posted to an Artillery Regiment that was in the process of being reorganized after suffering many casualties in the western desert. I was given command of a troop of guns. My senior gun number one (detachment commander) who could just about read and write, taught me how to strip and service the gun. A fellow troop commander, Ralph Settatree, who had previously worked in a bank, taught me man-management and how to administer the troop. My battery commander, a solicitor by profession and Territorial Army Officer, Maj Dick Peters, was kind and understanding. Norman Harding, previously a jeweller, was the Battery Captain. I owe a great deal to Dick Peters and Norman Harding, both of whom guided and taught me the basic essentials of command.

We were part of the 8 Indian Division located in northern Iraq. The Division was training for its coming role in Italy. The Divisional Commander, Russell 'Pasha', capable and personable, was popular with the rank and file. Many years later in 1949 I met Russell 'Pasha' when he was adviser to the Chief of Army Staff, Gen Cariappa. Unfortunately, Cariappa did not exploit Pasha's full potential. As a General Staff Officer at Army Headquarters, I had often gone to him for advice and had always come back wiser and better-informed. He was unfailingly courteous and I learned a great deal from Russell 'Pasha'. He talked about the time when he attended a planning conference for the capture of the islands of Cos and Leros. The planners maintained that since the numbers of Italians and Germans on the islands were about equal, they would neutralize each other and that the 8 Indian Division would have little trouble in taking the islands. At the fag end of the meeting the Admiral conducting the discussions turned to

Russell for his views. Russell, who did not agree with a word that had been said so far replied, 'Gentlemen, I stopped reading the brothers Grimm at the age of twelve.'

My troop was affiliated to the 1/5th Royal Gurkha Rifles. The Battalion was commanded by Lt Col Briggs. 'Briggo' as he was called was a father figure and well liked. Unfortunately, he was hard of hearing and when verbal orders were issued I would note the points and brief him later. The 17 Infantry Brigade was commanded by Brig Jenkins. The Brigade was ordered to construct defences in northern Iraq as the intelligence anticipated a possible German thrust to the Kirkuk oilfields. I was deputed to join the Brigade and plan artillery support and anti-tank defences. I was only a Second Lieutenant but was determined not to be overawed. I arrived with my troop at the location, did a thorough reconnaissance and reported to the Brigade Orders Group. Brig Jenkins asked me what I thought of the proposed defensive layout. With the brashness of youth I said, 'Sir, your defensive layout is unsound as it is not based even on a partial anti-tank obstacle.' Pointing to a piece of broken ground he asked, 'What about that?' I said 'a couple of rounds of 75 mm tank gun fire would be sufficient to clear it'. There was dead silence for a minute before Jenkins replied, 'Well gunner, what do you suggest?' I replied that there was a *wadi* a few hundred yards to the rear that could, with a little effort, be developed into an anti-tank obstacle. Jenkins then said, 'Briggo, go and have a look.' My suggestion was accepted. My self-confidence received an enormous boost. Jenkins was a capable commander, liked by all. It was unfortunate that later in Italy he was removed from command by Montgomery, who had little liking for Indian Army Officers, on the grounds that Jenkins was too old. Incidentally, at Sandhurst, Montgomery had applied for the Indian Army but did not pass out high enough to qualify!

We trained with Glubb's Arab Legion, a competent, well trained force. The Iraqi troops located in this area were ill-trained and lacked discipline but the Polish Carpathian Division commanded by Gen Anders was also stationed nearby and proved to be a far more hospitable place. I met Anders a few times and was impressed by his dedication. I got to like the Kurds in the area too, even though they often took pot shots at us for fun from a distance.

The Regiment was unable to get the reinforcements or equipment it required and we were, therefore, ordered to return to India to reform and re-equip, a decision that left most of us terribly disappointed. At first we were asked to take the land route through Iran and Afghanistan. However, this plan was soon dropped as our vehicles were also required to be left behind. We went back by sea to Karachi and thence to Sialkot. We were soon re-equipped and made up to strength, but instead of returning to the middle-east we were sent to the jungles near Ranchi for jungle warfare training. I was deputed for a short time to Stilwell's Chinese forces which were being trained at Ramgarh nearby. We were part of the 26 Indian Division of the XV Indian Corps. The Corps Commander was Gen 'Bill' Slim. Slim was extremely popular with all: he was practical, humane and knew how to handle men. He talked freely to everyone and did not stand on protocol. Slim was soon promoted to command the XIV Army. The XV Corps was to come directly under Headquarters Allied Land Forces South-East Asia. Lt Gen Christison replaced Slim in the XV Corps. We were disappointed as Christison was not of the same calibre as Slim. The Regiment, as part of the 26 Indian Division, served in operations in the Arakan Theatre of Burma. The Division fought with distinction in the various battles in the dense jungles of the Mayu range and in the numerous amphibious operations down the Arakan coast. After the capture of Ramree Island, where I was wounded in a Japanese air attack, elements of the Division sailed to Madras on the troop-ship MV *Dunera* for a well-deserved period of rest. However, when we reached Madras all ranks were ordered to go on a route march with full equipment through the streets of the city. Soon after reboarding, the troop ship sailed out to sea. We were terribly disappointed as the promised period of rest did not materialize. No one knew where we were bound until the outline of Ramree Island became visible. On anchoring we were visited by the new Divisional Commander, Maj Gen Chambers. Chambers, who had been Brigadier General Staff at the XV Corps Headquarters, and who apparently had the confidence of the Corps Commander, replaced Maj Gen Lomax, the popular commander of the Division. Chambers decided to address all ranks on the deck. A long and inappropriate pep talk followed. There was much fidgeting and coughing, particularly from the other ranks of a British battalion of the Linconshire Regiment. Chambers had barely begun to outline our future role when the British other ranks started spontaneous barracking followed by boos and catcalls. Chambers climbed down the gangway into the launch alongside amidst further boos and hisses. The British officers of the Battalion did not seem inclined to check the men. Soon after disembarking we were visited by many staff officers from the XV Corps trying to ascertain the state of morale. Lord Louis Mountbatten visited and went around speaking to the men in an attempt to rectify the situation. Years later, in the summer of 1960, when I met Lord Mountbatten at Fort Bragg in the USA, he remembered the incident at Ramree and said that the high command had indeed been worried. He then recounted the serious lack of coordination between the planners and the intelligence for this operation. The initial plan had been for an assault on the Andaman Islands. Intelligence were told, as part of the cover plan, to simulate a attack on Ramree Island. The plan was then changed and Ramree Island itself became the objective. This, however, was not passed on to the intelligence, who continued to simulate an attack on Ramree Island. Fortunately for us, they simulated the attack some miles south of the area of our actual landing, on the beaches off Mount

Peter. Mountbatten was charming and talked a great deal on various subjects. Besides the nostalgic memories of his campaign in Burma, he talked of his love for India and looked back with pride on his tenure as the Supreme Commander, South-East Asia Command.

Rangoon was soon occupied by the 26 Indian Division, the Japanese having vacated it a few days earlier. The Division then returned to India for a rest and refit in the area of Bangalore prior to Operation 'Zipper', the code name for the assault on Malaya. However, with the dropping of the atomic bombs on Hiroshima and Nagasaki, Japan surrendered. Shortly after the surrender the Division was ordered to Sumatra to disarm the Japanese and repatriate prisoners of war and civilians, both men and women, from the various prison camps. The Regiment landed at Belawan and moved on to Medan. At first the local inhabitants were very friendly but soon changed their attitude when they realized that we meant not only to disarm the Japanese but to reinstall the Dutch as their rulers. Our men in the Regiment, all Punjabi Mussalmans who sympathized with the Indonesians, were also unhappy with the task they had been allotted. Many British officers too, felt the same way. Long and protracted counter-insurgency operations followed; casualties were relatively high, particularly with the 6 Rajputana Rifles, who had four officer casualties over a short period. In one particular operation Maj Sabnis, who was moving with me, took a burst of small arms fire in his stomach.

Turco Westerling, half Turk, half Dutch, was the intelligence officer of the Division. It was alleged by the locals that he was brutal and cruel. They had posted a reward of 20,000 US dollars for his capture, dead or alive. Westerling and I had clashed on a few occasions. I recall one particular incident when he tried to force his way, without authorization, past one of my perimeter posts. I told the post commander, a havildar, to stop him. The havildar did this most enthusiastically with the butt of his rifle. Westerling was soon replaced by a British Intelligence Officer. The new officer, accompanied by four sergeants marched in and asked the post commander to let them though as they had proper authorization to go across to the plantation to check on the reported military build up. I warned them not to be so foolhardy. However, they brushed aside my advice and ventured into the plantation. That was the last I saw of them. Three days later the body of the officer was found dumped on the other side of the bridge. Years later Westerling was again in the news. This time he had gathered around him some Ambonese and raised a revolt against Indonesia. Westerling had a remarkable capacity for landing himself in the most controversial situations.

The Headquarters Allied Forces in South-East Asia allotted a few vacancies to those whom they considered deserving to be flown to Bali for a short rest. I was fortunate to be one of the dozen selected. We were flown in DC 3 transport together with a jeep and trailer. We landed on a grass airstrip at Denpasar. The pilot told us to meet him at the same place 14 days later. Bali was out of this world, relaxed and uninhibited, the women clad in the traditional manner. The vibrant Balinese culture, art, music and dance, suffused the place. There were no troops, no police, just happy contented people. I spent most of my days with a Belgian artist, Le Mayeur. He was married to a lovely Balinese woman, Pollock, who was the model for his vibrant paintings. Le Mayeur's style was reminiscent of Gaugin. The bungalow on the beach where Mayeur lived, together with its collection, is now a museum.

On the return trip from Bali the Air Force crew loaded the plane with live pigs to take back to their base. Half-way through one of the engines failed and the pigs and other non-essentials had to be dumped by the crew. We managed to maintain height and were able to land at an intermediate field. After some repairs we were on our way.

We left Medan in November 1946. While we were handing over our part of the perimeter to the Dutch, the Indonesians started firing from a distance. Our vehicles were lined up to take us to the anchorage at Belawan, where our ship was waiting to take us back to Madras. We departed under a hail of fire. Fortunately, no one was hurt.

On arrival in India the Regiment proceeded to Ranchi, while I received orders to depart for the United Kingdom to do a Gunnery Staff course at Larkhill. Set in the midst of the wind-swept Salisbury plain, the winter of 1946-7 at Larkhill was particularly cold. There were the usual post-war shortages to contend with: no heating in the mess and severely rationed food. Despite these limitations I enjoyed my stay. Though we had to work hard on the course we were able to travel during the weekends. I managed a short fishing trip to Scotland and a few memorable days in Paris before sailing back to India.

I returned to an independent India on 19 August 1947 and reported to the School of Artillery at Deolali. The School was commanded by Brig 'Fatty' Frowen, who had lost one leg in the Western Desert and had been captured by the Germans. Legend has it that during the ding dong battles that followed, he was freed. Later, when he was introduced to Gen Montgomery, Monty demanded of him the reason for his being taken prisoner. Frowen replied, 'Sir, you too would had been taken prisoner had you left a leg behind.'

The School of Artillery was going through a critical phase. The assets of the School were in the process of being divided between India and Pakistan. As the British instructors had decided to leave, only two qualified gunnery instructors remained: Maj M R Apte and myself. We had been together for the course at Larkhill in England and had served in the same Regiment during the War. Apte was given charge of the young officers' course. I was assigned the Gunnery Staff course, a course designed to provide instructors in gunnery for the Artillery. The students included some who had opted to serve with the Pakistan Army. They left for Pakistan after a few weeks.

I enjoyed my three-year tenure at Deolali, after which I had a short spell at Army Headquarters before moving on to the Staff College at Wellington. On completion of the course I was sent to take command of the Patiala Mountain Battery. This Battery had previously been part of the State Forces and had now been amalgamated into the Indian Army. It was located first at Tangdhar in Kashmir, and later at Poonch and Rajouri. Command of a mountain battery is perhaps one of the finest experiences one can expect as a major. I had always loved horses. I got to love the mules as well. A mountain battery in those days was equipped with the 3.7 inch howitzer, a successor to Kipling's screw gun. There were four officers, some two hundred and seventy-five men, twenty-five chargers and ninety-six mules. Hardly had I completed two years in command than I was assigned to the 1 Armoured Division as Brigade Major Artillery. In May 1956 I was ordered to raise a new Field Regiment, the 3 Field, in Delhi. We started from scratch. After six months the Regiment was exercised and declared fit for combat. We then moved to Ambala to join the 4 Infantry Division, commanded by Maj Gen B M Kaul whose only previous regimental service was with the Army Service Corps. His family connections with the Nehrus and his association with the Defence Minister, Krishna Menon, made him arrogant and arbitrary. I had to organize a firepower demonstration for a high-powered visiting Chinese Military delegation which went off fairly well. However, my relations with the General remained strained as I would not form part of the circle of confidants and sycophants which he was in the process of recruiting. Several confrontations followed. Fortunately, I was posted to the Headquarters in Delhi and Rajasthan area as General Staff Officer Grade 1 before more serious problems could arise.

My tenure in Delhi and Rajasthan was interesting, both professionally and socially. In 1958-9, there was an outbreak of hepatitis in Delhi due to the pollution of the water supply and we were asked to aid the civil authorities. I was summoned by the Defence Minister, Krishna Menon, and ordered to take charge of the water supply of Delhi. I told him that I had no expertise in running the water supply of a city. He replied sarcastically that I could learn. Fortunately, we had in Delhi at that time an Engineer, Electrical and Maintenance Company commanded by Lt Col Lakshmanan. We visited the Wazirabad waterworks and located the cause of the trouble. The intake for the water supply was only 50 yards upstream of the channel for discharge of effluents. After corrective action had restored normalcy we tried, unsuccessfully, to hand over the water supply back to the civil authorities. Later, Krishna Menon accompanied by the Army Chief, Gen Thimayya, visited the project. As we had been running this project for some six months, I asked the Chief to request the minister to have the water supply handed back to the civil authorities. Thimayya, who was not on the best of terms with Krishna Menon told me to tell him directly. I requested Krishna Menon accordingly. He did not reply. After a pause of a few seconds I repeated the request; he remained silent. I repeated the request a third time. Krishna Menon turned angrily on me and snapped, 'Colonel, I heard you the first time.' However, a couple of days later we received orders to hand the water supply back to the civil authorities.

Around this time I was also ordered to carry out trials with the 5.56 mm Armalite small arms range of weapons. The Army needed a replacement for the bolt action .303 rifle. The system performed well and was recommended by us. Strangely enough, the Armalite was not found suitable by the General Staff as it could not produce a four-inch group from a hundred yards and thus failed to measure up to one of the General

Staffs' requirements. Later, the General Staff finally rejected it as it was not considered suitable for ceremonial drills. Later, the Indian version of the FN Rifle was selected. Some thirty years after the Army accepted a similar, indigenously designed, light weight rifle of the same calibre and similar performance.

In August 1959 I was selected to attend the Advanced Artillery and Missile course at Fort Sill, Oklahoma, and Fort Bliss, Texas. Before departing, I was called by Krishna Menon for a briefing. He signalled me to sit down, glanced through some papers and offered me a cup of tea and some biscuits. Krishna Menon had visited us several times earlier and each time his staff had insisted that the minister be served imported English biscuits with his tea. I do remember the difficulties the mess Secretary had in trying to get English biscuits. I picked up the biscuit offered to me by the minister and looked at it and him before biting it. It was a perfectly good Indian biscuit and he was also nibbling one. I smiled and got a filthy look in return. A long anti-American tirade followed. When he finished I remarked that, if he felt that way about the USA, why did he have to send anyone to that country at all? Another angry tirade followed, after which he asked me to leave.

Before leaving I had to make arrangements for the two year old leopard that I had reared from a cub as well as get rid of my MG sports car. I was sorry to part with both. While passing through Bombay I met Gen Kaul who was surprised to see me on my way to the USA. I told him that if he wished to have me taken off the course I would not appeal. He scowled angrily but took no action. I spent an interesting year with the United States Army. I reported to the Field Artillery and Missile School at Fort Sill, where I was told to proceed to the Air Defence School at Fort Bliss on the outskirts of El Paso. The curriculum included air defence, missiles and use of radar and electronic equipment of which I had no previous experience and I had to work hard to keep pace. After three months at Fort Bliss, we went back to Fort Sill.

A large proportion of the American officers who had opted for the course were from the Reserve Officers Training Corps (ROTC). The American involvement in the Vietnam war meant that large numbers of officers had to be trained quickly. This naturally affected the quality of instruction as priority was given to quantity rather than quality. The American system of military education was, also, quite different from what we had been used to: small classes and individual attention, with the aim of training instructors for teaching establishments and units. There were numerous tests. The results were posted for all to see. There were students from many nations friendly to the USA. National pride spurred me on to aim for a high percentage. I finished the course with an overall percentage well into the nineties. On leaving the School, in token of my appreciation, I presented it a mounted leopard skin. Unfortunately, one of the teeth had been damaged during transit. I took the mounted skin and head to a dentist in Lawton. At first, he feigned umbrage and said that restoring a leopard's tooth was an insult to his profession and declined to help. However, on my agreeing to pay the exorbitant charge he later quoted the leopard's tooth was restored.

Sailing from New York to Southampton aboard the Queen Mary, and from there to Bombay on an Anchor Line ship, I reached India in August 1960. Ocean voyages in those days were relaxed, pleasurable journeys. During the day we spent our time taking part in various deck games and relaxing by the swimming pool. Dinners were formal, black tie affairs. Back in India I spent a few months as Chief Instructor, Tactics, at the School of Artillery before taking up the assignment of General Staff Officer Operations at Headquarters Western Command in November 1960. Western Army was then commanded by Lt Gen Thapar, who was later to take over as Chief of the Army Staff prior to the fateful Chinese invasion of 1962.

I had differences on concepts pertaining to the defence of Ladakh with the Army Commander and his Chief of Staff, Maj

Gen Gopal Bewoor and sometimes the exchanges between us became heated. I stressed allotting greater priority to building up the infrastructure, particularly the roads. Brig Prem Chand, the Brigadier General Staff, was a competent officer and stood by me. Fortunately, before long I was asked by Maj Gen Manekshaw to proceed as an instructor to the Defence Services Staff College on a three year tenure. Wellington is a well-organized military station. I lived in the Wellington Club. The workload as an instructor was heavy and the social commitments exacting. However, the sports facilities were incomparable and made up for all other shortcomings: golf, tennis, squash, horseback riding, amateur horse racing and fishing for trout in the mountains and mahseer in the plains. Fishing had always been my joy.

Some of the teachings and exercises at the Staff College were outdated. I remember, in particular, the mountain warfare series which I had to update. The exercise was set in the North-West Frontier and based on defunct British Indian Army tactics of picketing in the North-West Frontier. I reset the exercise in the area of Bomdi La which, coincidentally, became the scene of fighting during the Chinese invasion of 1962. As a result of my failure to oblige Gen Kaul in giving evidence against Manekshaw, I was not given command of an infantry brigade for the operations, but was sent on a staff assignment to Southern Command at Poona. After Kaul had left the Army, I was given command of an Artillery Brigade in Ladakh.

A two year tenure in Ladakh followed. This high altitude desert was then one of the loveliest, unspoiled areas on this planet. The air was clean and clear, the people uninhibited. I travelled widely, visited the numerous monasteries and studied Buddhist culture. The wild life was a pleasure to watch: ibex, wild sheep, wild asses, the 'chukor' or Asiatic partridge, the beautifully coloured snow pheasant and the very rare and seldom seen snow leopard.

There was an old Moravian mission at Leh in the grounds of

which had been planted the Lombardy poplar. I encouraged the troops to plant poplar and the local willow. I used to distribute cuttings at the various Army locations I visited. I like to think that I, too, have contributed to the greater greenery to be seen around Ladakh. We worked on making a golf course on sandy soil at an altitude of twelve thousand feet. The 'greens' were stabilized with old engine oil and the ball had to be placed on a mat on the sandy fairways.

My next assignment was at the School of Artillery as Commandant (1965-6). Deolali has always had a special place in my heart. As I took charge, war clouds began to gather and the situation in the border areas of Rajasthan, Gujarat and Jammu & Kashmir began to deteriorate. As war with Pakistan broke out, the Chinese threatened to intervene. Unfortunately, we withdrew from the crest line on the Jelap La and the Chinese immediately occupied it.

The 1965 war with Pakistan was indecisive, producing no winner. My next assignment was to command an Infantry Brigade at Samba, on the border of Jammu with Pakistani Punjab. We were soon involved in numerous border incidents. My Pakistani counterpart was Brig Azmat Hyat, a thorough gentleman. We held regular meetings to demarcate the border. His Government would not allow permanent concrete pillars as boundary markers so we dug in earth filled petrol drums as border markers. I learned a great deal in command of this brigade. We regularly took the whole brigade group out on cross-country manoeuvers with tanks and artillery. In 1967 I was promoted to Maj Gen and sent to command an Infantry Division in Rajasthan. The Division was in the process of being formed and came directly under Command Headquarters. The Army Commander, Lt Gen Moti Sagar, was a competent and upright soldier who had earlier been my platoon commander when I was an officer cadet at Mhow. He gave me a free hand to train my command.

I made a study of desert warfare and was fortunate in being

allowed to exercise the Division. Over a period of time I evolved concepts of operating in the desert, based on selection of the type of objective and the bypassing of opposition. The objectives were to be communication centres. The Indian Army was to a large extent, road-bound and had been trained to move along a road axis. We trained to move off the main axis to the objective. The opening of an axis of maintenance was left until a later stage. We had no navigational devices. I developed a simple but reliable method using the issue compass mounted on a gimbal, together with, specially prepared magnetic variation graph of the navigational vehicle employed. This gave an accuracy of 200 metres over a distance of 50 kilometres. The system I developed is still in use. My manual on desert warfare was used later to prepare the Army Headquarters manual on the subject. We also prepared the first terrain 'going' maps of the area, indicating the suitability of the various areas for the movement of wheeled and tracked vehicles.

In April 1969 I received a phone call from Lt Gen Manekshaw, telling me that he was moving to Army Headquarters as Chief of the Army Staff and that he was having me posted as Chief of Staff, Eastern Command at Calcutta. He said that he knew that I did not like to work as his staff officer, since earlier I had requested him not to have me posted as his Brigadier General Staff, but that I would have to work with him for about two weeks, which should pose no great problem. I moved into the Water Gate House at Fort William. This lovely house had been built on the ramparts of Fort William over the Water Gate around 1780. The water from the river Hoogly was drawn from the river to flood the moat of the Fort. It was a historic and lovely house with rooms of massive proportions. The view of the river from the lawns on the ramparts was breathtaking. I was back in the Calcutta of my birth, a Calcutta where I had spent my early years and a Calcutta I loved. It was the Calcutta I like to remember, a Calcutta of friendly people, cultured and warm.

Prelude to War

I settled down to work as Chief of Staff, Eastern Command, in May 1969. One of the first problems we had to tackle was that of insurgencies in Nagaland, Manipur and Mizoram. We already had major forces deployed on the Himalayan border with China. Then, there were the law and order problems in West Bengal caused by Naxalite activists and the Army had to be called in to assist the civil administration in countering their terrorist activities. Elections to the State Assembly were due and in spite of initial reluctance on my part to oversee security for the elections, ultimately the Army had to be deployed to protect polling stations. Even though the Naxalite movement was eventually contained in West Bengal, and its influence substantially eroded, in the north-east insurgencies continued to gain momentum and Army operations did not seem to be producing the desired results. It was as if the movements were becoming uncontrollable. Lacking jungle mobility, troops were committed largely to manning stationary posts as they were, for the most part, road bound. I did try to persuade our commanders to alter their tactics, but met with little success.

Meanwhile, momentous events were unfolding in East Pakistan.

The two wings of Pakistan, the East and the West, separated geographically by a thousand miles of Indian territory, differed greatly in size and density of population. In area, West Pakistan was almost six times as large as the East.

However, according to the 1961 census, its population was forty-three million as against fifty-one million in East Pakistan. There were differences in language, culture, and outlook. An additional factor was the sizable Hindu population of over ten million in East Pakistan. The people of East Pakistan felt that they were being subjected to exploitation and 'internal colonialism' and resented the fact that the West was developing with money earned by the East. In 1960, the per capita income in West Pakistan was 32 per cent higher than in the East, with a higher annual growth. Before long, Bengali nationalism surged and in 1966 Sheikh Mujibur Rehman announced his 'Six Point Programme' for provincial autonomy in matters other than foreign affairs and defence (see Appendix 11).

In 1967 Sheikh Mujibur Rehman and others were charged with formenting a secessionist movement with Indian support, in what came to be known as the Agartala Conspiracy Case. The trial that started in Dacca in 1969 made a hero out of Mujib and his popularity soared high. President Ayub Khan called a round table conference in Rawalpindi in March 1969 and, with the Conspiracy Case withdrawn, Mujib was invited to attend. However, the conference failed and Ayub Khan resigned, declaring 'I am left with no option but to step aside and leave it to the defence forces of Pakistan, which today represent the only effective and legal instrument to take over full control of the affairs of the country.' Gen Yahya Khan, the Army Chief, then took over.

In November 1969 Yahya Khan announced that elections based on universal suffrage would take place at the end of 1970. Sheikh Mujib's Awami League won 160 seats in the National Assembly, taking all but 2 seats in the East, though none in the West. Bhutto's Pakistan People's Party won 81 seats out of 138 in the West, that too mainly in Punjab and Sind. The Awami League's victory reflected the strength of Bengali nationalism and the deep resentment against the social and economic dominance of the East by the West. Bhutto, however, was quick to exploit the fears of the West regarding political domination by East Pakistan. He bitterly opposed the 'Six Point Programme' of the Awami League and tried to work out a formula which would ensure that he could at least share power with Mujib.

Yahya Khan vacillated about summoning the National Assembly. In January 1971 he visited Dacca to try and reach an agreement with Mujib that would guarantee a role for the defence forces, and his own position as President. On returning to West Pakistan he referred to Mujib as 'the future Prime Minister', but even then did not announce a date for the convening of the Assembly. At the end of January Bhutto went to Dacca in an attempt to work out an arrangement with Mujib, but with little success.

Meanwhile, a secret reinforcement of troops from West Pakistan to the East via Sri Lanka began. On 1 March Yahya Khan announced that the meeting of the National Assembly had been postponed *sine die* and that Maj Gen Yakub Khan had been appointed the new Governor of East Pakistan. The Awami League reacted with a campaign of civil disobedience. Yahya then announced that the National Assembly would meet on 25 March. He also announced that he was replacing Yakub Khan by Lt Gen Tikka Khan (who had displayed a particular ruthlessness in suppressing the civil disorders in Baluchistan). All the while the reinforcement of troops continued—perhaps calculations about Indian reactions had no place in what the Pakistanis regarded as their internal problem.

When Yahya arrived in Dacca on 15 March, once again the negotiations concerning the nature of the transfer of power to the Assembly and the 'Six Point Programme' floundered. Bhutto claimed that if power were to be transferred before adopting a new constitution, as required by Mujib, it should be transferred simultaneously to the majority party in each wing. On 22 March the Awami League accepted this suggestion but later the Army made it out to be a virtual constitutional formula for secession. Hasan Zaheer, in his book *The Separation of East Pakistan: The Rise and Realization of Bengali Muslim Nationalism*, asserts that even as he held negotiations with the Awami League, Yahya Khan

was visiting army installations and meeting army officers in the cantonment . . . after every visit and meeting he came back with a more aggressive attitude towards political settlement and with an over-simplified view of the army's capability to control affairs. He was heavily influenced by the top brass that he need not or should not concede too much to the politicians.

When it was decided that the meeting of the National Assembly should again be postponed demonstrations took place in Dacca and in the smaller towns. On Pakistan Day, i.e. 23 March, Bangladesh flags were hoisted all over, and independence was proclaimed.

Late in the afternoon of 25 March the confusion ended with Yahya Khan flying back to West Pakistan via Colombo Earlier, Tikka Khan had issued orders for a crackdown to commence at 0100 hours on 26 March (on the estimate that by then the President would be back in Karachi). Troops began to move from the cantonment into the city at 2300 hours on 25 March, and firing commenced before the scheduled hour of 'Operation Searchlight'. A message from Sheikh Mujibur Rehman was then heard that evening on the radio, proclaiming the People's Republic of Bangladesh. He said, 'This may be my last message. From today Bangladesh is independent. I call upon the people of Bangladesh to resist the Army of occupation to the last. Your fight must go on until the last soldier of the Pakistan occupation Army is expelled from the soil of Bangladesh and final victory is achieved.'

Dacca was brought under the control of the Pakistani Army in just a few hours. The casualties were estimated at several thousand. Mujib was arrested at 1.00 a.m. on 26 March 1971 at his residence in Dhanmandi and flown to Karachi three days later, but most other Bengali leaders escaped. Foreign journalists were confined to the Intercontinental Hotel, to be deported by 27 March.

Resistance was heavy, particularly at the Dacca University. The Pakistanis used tanks, rocket launchers, recoilless guns and mortar to take the University building. Bhutto left Dacca after congratulating the Army for 'saving Pakistan'. Even so, the situation remained fluid. Maj Ziaur Rehman, the second-in-command of the 8 East Bengal Regiment took over the command of forces in Chittagong and on 27 March seized the transmitting station and broadcast his declaration of independence. This was heard by many and passed on by word of mouth to those who hadn't.

The Pakistani Army in the East at the time of the crackdown consisted of four Infantry Brigades. This force was rapidly built up in the succeeding months to thirty-five regular Infantry Battalions. There were seven wings of Para-military forces from the West, seven wings of East Pakistan civil armed forces, several Companies of the Industrial Protection Force and large numbers of irregulars, Mujahids and Razakars. The Artillery consisted of six field regiments, several independent field and heavy mortar batteries and light anti-aircraft artillery. The armour component comprised one regiment of American Chaffee tanks, one independent squadron of Chaffee tanks and one mixed squadron of Chaffee and Russian PT 76 tanks. The Air Force was equipped with twenty-five Sabre jet fighters, transport aircraft and some helicopters, and the Navy with a number of gunboats.

As for Bengali troops, there were five East Bengal Battalions officered mainly by Bengali officers, and the East Pakistan Rifles manned by Bengalis. There were a number of Bengali Mujahids, Ansars, and Civil Police. The Pakistani

Army had taken care to see that these were well dispersed before the crackdown.

Maj Zia resisted the Pakistani Army in Chittagong with all available Bengali regular and para-military forces. Heavy fighting erupted in the Headquarters of the East Pakistan Rifles, where the Pakistani Army used tanks, aircraft, artillery and fire from Naval gunboats. The position was captured on 31 March. The next assault was on the Reserve Police lines, which fell without much resistance. Zia then fell back towards Belonia, blowing up the strategic Feni road bridge which connected Dacca with the port of Chittagong.

Meanwhile, the 1 East Bengal from Jessore had several initial successes against Pakistani troops. There was heavy fighting around Kushtia town and casualties were inflicted on the Pakistanis. At Pabna, too, the East Pakistan Rifles Wing had initial successes. Another battalion, the 2 East Bengal, located at Joydebpur, north of Dacca, with elements in Tangail and Mymensingh, moved north after sporadic fighting.

By 18 April, however, the 1 East Bengal had evacuated Chuadanga, the provisional capital of Bangladesh, and fallen back with some Border Security elements to the Indian border at Bangaon.

The repercussions of the Pakistani crackdown, meanwhile, were being felt in India. As the actual situation came to be known, there was a public outcry and demands for immediate intervention. On 31 March the Indian Parliament passed a resolution calling on Pakistan to 'transfer power to the legally elected representatives of the people of East Bengal' (see Appendix 13). The country was shocked at the scale of Pakistani atrocities because of which refugees were pouring into India. What began as a trickle in late March was to become a steady stream between April and June, and to continue until October.

At the beginning of April, Gen S H F J Manekshaw, the

Army Chief, called on the telephone to say that the Government required Eastern Command to move immediately into East Pakistan. I protested that this was impractical. We had at our disposal only Mountain Divisions trained for mountain operations. They had virtually no bridging equipment and their transport capabilities for movement in the plains were severely limited. There were several large, wide, tidal rivers between Calcutta and Dacca. On the other side of Bangladesh, Agartala was vulnerable, with just a garrison of one infantry battalion to protect it. Because of tenuous communications in this region, it would require considerable time to reinforce. We would also need time to suitably equip and retrain our mountain troops for operations in riverine terrain. This was imperative because the coming monsoon and rice paddies would make access to the unbridged rivers extremely difficult. If we moved now, we could at best reach the Padma. Further, international opinion at that time was not supportive of Bangladesh's quest for independence. The international press were not yet convinced of the atrocities committed on the people of East Pakistan.

Gen Manekshaw then asked by what date we would be ready. Provided we got bridging and suitable weapons and equipment, I said, we could be ready earliest by 15 November. This would leave adequate time after the monsoon for the terrain to become passable. Manekshaw, upset and impatient, replied that he would get back to me.

Gen Manekshaw called again the next day, sounding very agitated, to say that senior bureaucrats in the Government were accusing the Army of being over-cautious, if not cowardly. He said we should reconsider. I reiterated my views and suggested that he could, if he so wished, tell the Government that it was the Eastern Command who were dragging their feet. This led to an outburst of invective. Even so, it is to the credit of Gen Manekshaw that he had the courage to uphold our stand and inform Prime Minister

Indira Gandhi accordingly. (See Appendix 6 for full details of Manekshaw's account of his subsequent briefing of Indira Gandhi.)

Shortly afterwards, I was visited at my residence in Fort William by a delegation from the Border Security Force (BSF), headed by its Director General, K Rustomji. He was accompanied by Golok Mazumdar, (Deputy Inspector General), and Maj Gen Narinder Singh, seconded to the BSF. They were very excited. Rustomji said he was in a great hurry as he had much to do. Intrigued, I asked him what it was about. He told me that since the Eastern Command would not throw the Pakistanis out of East Pakistan, the Government had asked the BSF to do so. I thought that he was joking and laughed. But he replied in all seriousness that the object of his visit was to invite Eastern Command to send a contingent to the victory parade in Dacca that he intended to hold in about two to three weeks. The sky was suddenly illuminated by a brilliant flash across the river by the flames of an explosion at an oxygen plant. I was taken aback. I realized that they were serious and that they believed that they could achieve what the Army, with all its resources, could not.

I told Rustomji, whom I knew reasonably well from the days I was commanding the 12 Infantry Division in Rajasthan, that his forces would be thrown back in a couple of weeks. If he wanted to use his force to the best advantage, he should consider setting up bases to facilitate future operations in the swamps of the Sunderbans and the jungles of the Chittagong hills.

I do not intend to go into the details of the BSF 'incursion' into the then East Pakistan, but a single incident may be revealing. About a fortnight later there was a call from the Commanding Officer of the BSF Battalion from our border post at Bangaon on the Jessore road, to say that his forces had been surrounded a few miles inside and were about to be attacked by Pakistani tanks. I knew there were no Pakistani tanks in that area; the intention was only to involve us prematurely in the hostilities. I asked if a relief Army column could reach him safely, and he said it could. Thereupon I told him that if an Army column could reach him safely, by the same logic he could extricate himself too. I said that if he fell back with elements of the East Bengal Regiment and Rifles we would cover the last stages, if necessary, from inside the Indian territory. He said he would do so. We than ordered an Infantry Battalion to proceed to cover the final withdrawal from the area of the border post, and the force withdrew into India. According to published Pakistani sources, a total of six BSF personnel were captured, who were later paraded by the Pakistanis in Dacca. So much for the victory parade in Dacca!

As the 1 East Bengal and the para military forces of East Pakistan, with some elements of the BSF, were steadily driven back down the Jessore–Bangaon road, the pursuing Pakistani Army fired a few shells which landed on our side of the border. Accompanied by Capt Sandhu, I proceeded to the area and there met Tajuddin Ahmed, the Acting Prime Minister of Bangladesh who was to meet a British Member of Parliament at the customs post just across the border. Worried about his safety, we advised elements of the East Bengal Regiment to protect the area and the flag of Bangladesh that had been set up there. This flag flew throughout the struggle.

On 29 April Eastern Command was officially given the responsibility of assisting Bangladesh forces in their liberation struggle, and the BSF located on the border were placed under the command of the Eastern Army.

I have known K Rustomji as a competent and pragmatic officer and I do not know why he committed his forces, neither adequately trained nor equipped, to that operation. Perhaps he was under great pressure, perhaps he wanted the

BSF, which he did so much to shape, to earn their spurs. It may be that he was swayed by exaggerated reports of the nature of resistance to the Pakistani Army. In all fairness, it needs to be said that the BSF given tasks within their capabilities, performed these with dedication and competence. The BSF also played a significant role in the liberation of Bangladesh and their contribution was enormous. Due credit must be given to Rustomji and his men for what they achieved inspite of their initial setback.

Political Developments

The diplomatic offensive of the Pakistani Government directed at the international community stressed that events in East Pakistan were an internal affair. The British Government initially took a position almost similar to Pakistan's and the French followed suit. Among the Muslim countries, Iran, Indonesia, Malaysia and Turkey were quick to give their support to the Pakistanis. The Central Treaty Organization also called for non-interference. The Arab countries, particularly Saudi Arabia, also voiced their support for Pakistan. Egypt was more lukewarm in its attitude. Of the super-powers, the Soviet Union appealed to the Pakistani President for a political solution (see Appendix 14). Yahya Khan replied that the situation in East Pakistan was normal and criticized India. China, on the other hand, came out in support of a unified Pakistan (see Appendix 15). Most people interpreted this to mean merely political support without any military commitment though China continued to provide military equipment and economic assistance to Pakistan. Initially, the general attitude of the State Department of United States of America was for a peaceful accommodation. This was to change later with President Nixon's overview of the balance of power in the region and his tilt towards Pakistan.

Meanwhile, by the end of March 1971, a number of Bengali resistance leaders arrived in Calcutta. Prominent among them were Tajuddin Ahmed, Nazrul Islam,

1. Jack Jacob as an Officer Cadet in 1942

2. No. 1 Platoon 'A' Company Officers' Training School Mhow, 1942. Jack Jacob top row fifth ftom left, to his right 'Tappy' Raina

3. Field Marshal Sam Manekshaw

4. Lt Gen Jagjit Singh Aurora

5. Lt Gen Jack Jacob

Qamaruzzaman, Mansur Ali, Col M A G Osmani, and Wing Cmdr Khondkar. A Government-in-exile was soon formed and was housed in a bungalow on Theatre Road (Shakespeare Sarani). I attended the initial deliberations with Tajuddin and Nazrul Islam. They wanted to hold, in Baidyanath Tala or 'Mujibnagar' which was just across the border in East Pakistan, a parliamentary session of those members of Parliament who had already been elected and who had managed to escape to India. With no appreciable area of East Pakistan in their control and very few members of Parliament in India compounded by the absence of Mujib I suggested that they proclaim a Provisional Government. I gave them the example of the Free French Government and General de Gaulle during World War II. They asked me to prepare a draft declaration for them to work on, which I did and gave to Tajuddin. He in turn showed it to some legal luminaries in Calcutta and had it expanded and dressed in legal terms. The Declaration was finally issued on 17 April at Baidyanath Tala, just inside East Pakistan, at a function organized by the Border Security Force. Unfortunately, some foreign correspondents stayed behind and saw the BSF removing the chairs.

In the first week of April I instructed Col Khara, Colonel Intelligence, Eastern Command, to make contact with the Pakistani Deputy High Commission at Calcutta which was almost entirely staffed by Bengalis and sound them out on whether they would like to join the Bangladesh Government-in-exile. Col Khara succeeded in establishing contact with the High Commission through an intermediary and the staff agreed to come over provided they were guaranteed their future service, pay, allowances and pensions. In mid-April I met Tajuddin and Nazrul Islam in the presence of Rustomji and briefed all three in detail. Tajuddin agreed to furnish the required guarantees. Since the matter from this point onwards could be better handled by the BSF, I asked

Rustomji if he would like to take over. Rustomji agreed. The key personnel came over on 18 April. There were, however, to be repercussions of a different kind. Because of the sensitive nature of the task, we had not informed the Chain of Command about our initiative. Some days later, as the Prime Minister got to know the full facts of the incident, she conveyed to Gen Manekshaw her appreciation of what the Army had done. Manekshaw, who had been totally unaware of the incident, was taken off guard and demanded an explanation as to why he had not been informed. Aurora telephoned me late at night demanding to know why *he* had been kept in the dark. I told him that as it was a very sensitive matter we had informed no one for obvious reasons.

The decision made at the end of March 1971 to help the Mukti Bahini was confirmed publicly later by the Minister of External Affairs. On 29 July, in a statement to the Parliament, he said,

This Parliament had unanimously adopted a resolution pledging sympathy and support, and we are pursuing that resolution in the best possible manner and we are doing everything possible to lend support to the freedom fighters.

The nature and quality of the assistance given to freedom fighters has already been well-documented. Siddiq Salik, PRO to Gen Niazi, in his book, *Witness to Surrender*, writes that training camps were established to train a total of 100,000 guerrillas: 30,000 were organized to fight a conventional war and 70,000 to carry out guerrilla warfare. Robert Jackson, in his book, *South Asian Crisis*, states that from the beginning of May began the formation, training and arming of Bangladesh forces, and covert official support was extended to the Provisional Bangladesh Government to organize a guerrilla war in East Pakistan. Salik, summarizes the pattern of Mukti Bahini operations in three phases. In June and July the Mukti Bahini operated in border areas where Indian troops were close by to support them. Their main achievements included the blowing up of minor culverts and harassment. Over the next two months their exploits included ambushing Army convoys, raiding Police Stations, blowing up vital installations and sinking river craft all the way to Dacca. Over October and November, backed by Indian troops and Artillery, they mounted pressure on border outposts and fomented trouble in towns and cities. It is during this period, he states, that the Indian Army established some important bridgeheads which they used profitably during the war.

That assistance was given to the Mukti Bahini is widely known in India through the Bangladesh Government, the Pakistanis and through many thousands of ex-Mukti Bahini. However, the manner in which this training was imparted was flawed from the start since too much weightage was given to numbers. In the training period of three or four weeks only very basic skills could be taught. Moreover, training of junior leaders was given insufficient importance. Had training periods been longer and more emphasis placed on the training of junior leaders, the Mukti Bahini could have produced even better results.

The appointment of Col M A G Osmani as Military Advisor and Commander-in-Chief of the Bangladesh Forces on 14 April brought its own pressures to bear on the organization of the forces. Osmani, a retired regular officer of the Pakistan Army, had been associated with the East Bengal Battalions, and these were close to his heart. He was dedicated and totally committed to the independence of Bangladesh. However, his views were orthodox. He wanted to model his forces on the organization and tactics of the Pakistan Army. He had reservations on the raising and employment of guerrilla forces preferring to raise regular East Bengal Battalions and devoted more time to organizing and training them than the Mukti Bahini. Osmani had a soldierly bearing and went to extremes to project appearances of being spartan. He slept on a camp bed and used camp furniture even in his quarters in the bungalow at Calcutta. Yet, in matters of food, his tastes were Epicurean as he liked to dine as in peace time. On the occasions he dined with me I would serve him a *pucca* sahib's dinner which he appreciated: soup, a fish course, a roast with vegetables, dessert and a savoury followed by coffee.

In many ways, Osmani was able to have his way. The East Bengal Battalions that had withdrawn to peripheral areas were reformed. The 1, 3 and 8 East Bengal Battalions were moved north towards the Meghalaya border areas and the 2 and 4 East Bengal to the eastern periphery. Osmani was instrumental in having three more East Bengal Battalions raised, mainly from the newly trained freedom fighters and in forming Artillery Batteries. It was originally conjectured that the East Bengal Battalion and Mukti Bahini could liberate a sufficiently large area around Mymensingh, but Osmani opposed this, stating that he could muster more local support in the east. He had the battalions moved from the north to the east with which region he was familiar.

Osmani's second in command was Wing Cmdr Khondkar. Khondkar was a polished, pragmatic officer. He had a practical approach to problems and was able to grasp essentials besides being accessible and easy to work with.

We, in the Eastern Command, were of the opinion that war with Pakistan was likely to break out in November or December. As the flow of Hindu refugees increased, the camps constructed hastily for them were filled and new ones had to be set up. This flow of refugees was to swell to around nine million. Meanwhile, the Pakistan Army's atrocities on the Hindu population and Muslim dissidents reached horrific proportions. Massacres, rape and other atrocities have been documented extensively by the Bangladesh authorities. We continued to receive authentic reports of these killings but the international media was slow to be convinced of the scale of the atrocities. We realized that we needed to bring this human catastrophe to the attention of the international community.

Although the public relations of the defence and other ministries were located in Delhi, most of the foreign corespondents and the international radio and TV network reporters were operating out of Calcutta. They were unimpressed by press releases from Delhi. Brig Sethna, the Brigadier General Staff, was handling the Indian press correspondents, and I the international media. The London *Sunday Times* correspondent, Nicholas Tomalin, a seasoned war corespondent, was not satisfied with briefings and he decided to go into Bangladesh to see things for himself. His report drew the attention of the world to the terrible atrocities perpetrated by the Pakistani Army in East Bengal. Tomalin, a truly professional and brave war correspondent, was later killed on the Golan Heights reporting, as always, from the front. Sydney Schanberg of the *New York Times* and subsequently of *Killing Fields* fame, as well as Tony Clifton of *Newsweek* also produced authentic accounts of the atrocities. We assisted in sending in a BBC television team with Allan Hart, whose coverage highlighted the rampant killings. A team from Granada television headed by that very brave lady, Vanya Kewley, went in from Agartala into East Pakistan and shot some revealing footage. We sent Gita Mehta, along with the Granada crew, at the request of her father, Biju Patnaik. The National Broadcasting Corporation of American and the CBS also sent in their teams. Despite the official policy of the State Department, following President Nixon's tilt towards Pakistan, international opinion was outraged at the behaviour of the Pakistan Army, and support for an independent Bangladesh began to grow around the world, even in the USA. Bangladesh and India should give due credit to the contribution of the international media for their factual and objective reporting of events in Bangladesh's struggle for independence.

One of our major impediments was the lack of intelligence, both military and topographical. The maps we had were over fifty years old and out of date. We had to obtain current maps. We liaised with the East Bengal Regiment and the Mukti Bahini to procure these and managed to get all the map sheets we required except for one. We approached the Survey of India in Calcutta for help. They were most cooperative, though in the time frame available they were not able to reproduce the maps on the same grid we use in India. The Pakistani maps, though metric in scale, had different grid origins and were gridded in yards, whereas ours were gridded in metres. We took a decision that for future operations in Bangladesh we would use the reproduced Pakistani maps even though they would create some problems for the artillery. The Survey of India reproduced all the copies we required and they were distributed to the units. When hostilities did break out later, our troops had sufficient up-to-date maps. However, no lessons seemed to have been learnt from this episode, for during the Indian Army's intervention in Sri Lanka in 1987, operations were hampered due to lack of up-to-date maps.

We had to supplement our topographical information, obtained from the maps, with details about rivers, tides, crossings, ferries, bridges and bridging sites, rail and water communications. The engineers obtained topographical data from diverse sources to compile an accurate topographical manual. A friend who was in shipping and had served in East Pakistan gave us details of the anchorages of Khulna, Mangla, Chalna and the port of Chittagong. I also involved the Director of Naval Intelligence in all our discussions.

The Military Intelligence Directorate, who were controlling the signal intercept resources, provided us with very little intelligence. Whatever little intelligence was received from the Mukti Bahini required very careful evaluation. The Research and Analysis Wing (RAW) gave us next to nothing. We were unable to build up the order of battle and the deployment of the Pakistani Army in East Pakistan. Reinforcements were being flown in via Colombo, but we could neither identify nor place these. In April/May 1971, I brought this to the notice of the Director of Military Intelligence at the Army Headquarters, asking for the signal intelligence units in the east to be put under our control. He replied that the Command Headquarters was not competent to process what he called 'raw information' and that only after thorough evaluation by his Headquarters in Delhi could he pass pertinent information on to us. The situation was impossible. We could not work effectively without immediate access to signal intercepts, not only in the period prior to hostilities but also during the war itself when responses had to be immediate. I then spoke to Gen Manekshaw and promised that if the signal intelligence organization was placed under us I would ensure that copies of all intercepts would be passed to his Director of Military Intelligence. We would also pass relevant information to the other services. Manekshaw agreed and issued the necessary instructions. Eastern Command was thus the only Command to have Signal Intelligence placed directly under it and this enabled us to build up the complete Pakistani order of battle in the East and to read enemy intentions. During operations it enabled us to respond immediately to changing situations. We were also able to intercept traffic between East and West Pakistan.

Even with our obsolete equipment we managed to intercept high frequency (HF) and very high frequency (VHF) enemy radio networks. The direction finding equipment, however, was vintage, and we were unable to get accurate fixations of locations.

We redeployed the intercepting stations and set up a

communication network for dissemination of information. Direct telephonic communication was established from this Signal Headquarters to my desk. The officer commanding this organization, Lt Col P C Bhalla, was given the authority to approach me directly if necessary. This Signal Intelligence unit was capable of limited code breaking. Even though they had only little success with critical Army codes, they were able to break the Naval code. Whenever any intercept indicated either concentration of craft or movement of gunboats we passed it on to Advance Air Headquarters at Fort William for immediate counteraction. One particular intercept during the later stages of the war, which had in the normal course been passed on to Delhi, indicated a rendezvous of craft at Gupta Crossing on the Meghna river. Gen Manekshaw interpreted this to mean that the Pakistanis were attempting to go by sea to Burma and ordered us to broadcast that he knew what they were up to. I spoke to Maj Gen Inder Gill, the Director of Military Operations, telling him that the inference that the Pakistanis intended to go to Burma by sea lacked credence and that there was no intelligence to support it. Further, these were river craft and not sea-going vessels. I pointed out to Inder that if the broadcast was made it would compromise our code breakers. Inder agreed and said he would speak to Gen Manekshaw. He rang back saying that Sam was adamant, refusing to listen to reason, and insisted that the broadcast be made. The broadcast was made, and as a result the Pakistanis changed their Naval code so that we were not able to read any subsequent Naval radio traffic.

We were able to intercept radio traffic between both wings of Pakistan. On 1 December 1971 we intercepted a message from West to East Pakistan advising them of the warning sent to all Pakistani merchant shipping not to enter the Bay of Bengal. We passed this on to the three Service Headquarters, Army, Navy and Air Force, as also an intercept warning civil aircraft not to fly near the Indian borders. The evaluation of these intercepts should have given us prior warning of the Pakistani intention to bomb our airfields on 3 December. We also intercepted signals from the submarine *Ghazi*, off Sri Lanka, and on her entering the Bay of Bengal. These were passed on to the Navy, both in Delhi and Vishakhapatnam.

Higher Command and Organization for War

The Indian system of higher command is loose and decentralized. The Chiefs of Staff of the Army, Navy and Air Force chair the Chiefs of Staff Committee by rotation. The tenure of each appointment is dependent on the remaining service of the Chief who assumes the appointment. He has little say over the other two Services, which are autonomous. The role of the Chairman is therefore limited to a degree of coordination. Much, too, depends on the personality of the Services Chief and his equation with the Defence Minister and, to some extent, the Prime Minister. The Defence Secretary, an officer of the Indian Administrative Service, has no operational responsibility and is generally not briefed on operational plans.

Before the war with China there were two main operational Army Commands, Western and Eastern. Southern Command, originally a training command, was given operational responsibility in Rajasthan and Gujarat. The Army Commands are responsible for operational planning in their respective Theatres. To a large extent they are logistically self-contained and capable of sustaining operations for specified periods. The Eastern Command Headquarters is located at Fort William in Calcutta, but the Air Force Command Headquarters were located elsewhere. Initially, we, at the Eastern Command had to deal with two Air Force

Commands—the Eastern at Shillong, which was responsible for the north-east, and the Central, located at Allahabad, responsible for the area south of the Ganga. It was difficult enough dealing with one command located several hundred miles away, let alone another almost as distant. I foresaw problems in the conduct of air-land operations with such a set up. I, therefore, spoke to Gen Manekshaw but he declined to take up the matter because of his strained relations with the Air Chief. Fortunately, Air Chief Marshal P C Lal, Chief of the Air Staff, visited us at Fort William and I requested that the Air Force boundaries be redrawn so that we had only one Air Force Command Headquarters to deal with. I also pointed out the difficulties of dealing with Command Headquarters several hundred miles away and suggested the location of an advanced Air Force Headquarters at Fort William. P C Lal was a highly pragmatic, capable officer, down to earth and practical. He said he understood our difficulties and promised to help. Shortly afterwards he changed the boundaries as requested and ordered the formation of an Advanced Headquarters at Fort William. Had we put up these proposals through routine staff channels the readjustments may not have materialized as there was considerable friction between the Army and Air Force Chiefs of Staff. On the naval front, the Headquarters of the Eastern Fleet were located at Vishakhapatnam, while a liaison officer was attached to the Eastern Command Headquarters.

Manekshaw was an officer with an impressive bearing and commanding personality and had an excellent command over the English Language. He had been commissioned in the Frontier Force Regiment and seen action during the retreat in Burma. He had been wounded in the battle for the Sittang Bridge and had been awarded the Military Cross for gallantry.

It was at the Staff College that Sam Manekshaw faced the

most serious crisis of his Army career. Armies, Navies and Air Forces, not only in India but world-wide are plagued with jealousies, ambitions and petty rivalries. There are numerous examples of this in Western countries. Lt Gen B M Kaul, a self proclaimed nationalist who saw in Manekshaw a potential rival, started a campaign of vilification against him. Later he instigated an inquiry to be carried out against him for anti-national activities. Trivial incidents and off the cuff remarks quoted out of context were used to substantiate these charges. The allegations were absurd. During dinner one evening I was called to the telephone at the quarters of Lt Col Shinde, a fellow instructor at the college. The caller stated that he was speaking on behalf of Kaul and asked me to give evidence against Manekshaw. Apparently, some indiscrete remarks by Manekshaw made earlier, in the presence of Lt Col (later Lt Gen) 'Zoru' Bakshi and myself were construed as evidence of Sam being anti-national. As Zoru Bakshi was away on United Nations peace-keeping duties in the Congo and, therefore, not readily available, I was told that if I did give evidence, my future in the Army would be assured and that I would get any assignment in any part of the world I desired. I declined. The officer, whose identity I knew, then said that I should think it over because if I refused, my Army career could be in jeopardy. I replied that my answer was final. Manekshaw was indeed fortunate that Lt Gen Daulat Singh was the presiding officer of the inquiry. Daulat Singh was an officer of high integrity and did not succumb to pressures, despite the fact that Kaul was the favoured protege of the Defence Minister, Krishna Menon and Sam was exonerated. It was most unfortunate for India that Kaul, earlier an officer of the Army Service Corps, was able in 1962, with political backing, to command the forces in the North-East Frontier.

As Chief of Staff Eastern Command I arrived at Command Headquarters in May 1969, two weeks before Manekshaw left for Delhi to take over as Chief of Staff. Lt Gen Jagjit Singh Aurora replaced Manekshaw. The Chief of Staff at the Command Headquarters has a crucial role. He is responsible for operational planning, executing military operations, logistics and coordinating the various components of the staff, arms and service elements of the Headquarters. He is the pivot around which the Headquarters revolve. A Headquarters must work as a team. When I arrived, I found personal contact between various branches lacking. Notes and minutes were being circulated when a phone call or a walk down the corridor would have clarified matters. The olive green bureaucracy can be as frustrating as its civilian counterpart. Soon after, Brig Adi Sethna arrived as the Brigadier General Staff. Adi was affable, gregarious and able to talk to everyone, which was to prove a great asset. We got on well. We were also lucky to have Chajju Ram as the Brigadier in charge of Administration. Chajju was hard-working, reliable, thorough and conscientious—qualities, essential for his post. We also had as Colonel Intelligence, Col M S Khara, a serious and thorough Staff Officer, to organize the intelligence activities systematically and effectively.

Perhaps the most important role played during my tenure was by the Chief Engineer. We had asked for Brig 'Baba' Bhide. Fortunately, he arrived in time to organize the engineering effort for the upcoming operations against Pakistan. I made it clear to Bhide that his primary responsibility was bridging. This required detailed planning, obtaining the equipment, repairing and making bridges serviceable and most important their correct and timely placement. When hostilities did break out the bridging, so essential to movement, was placed where it was required and in almost all cases, in time. Much of the credit for our success in the operations in East Pakistan should go to Baba Bhide.

At Army Headquarters I worked with the Vice Chief, Lt Gen Har Prasad and the Director of Military Operations, first Maj Gen K K Singh (who was promoted to command a Corps in August 1971) and subsequently with Maj Gen Inder Gill, a thoroughly competent, outspoken, blunt and down to earth man without whose support and understanding it would have been well nigh impossible for me to have functioned effectively.

Evolution of Plans

The land of East Bengal is low-lying, water-logged, and intersected by numerous rivers. The rivers, very wide and generally flowing from north to south become tidal in the lower reaches. A large part of the terrain is swampy. The cultivable area is intersected by bunds demarcating the numerous small holdings devoted to the cultivation of rice and jute. In the hill areas, to the east, some tea is cultivated. The monsoon generally sets in at the end of May and withdraws by the end of September. The heavy rains in the catchment areas of the rivers in the north cause floods and widen the rivers at places to several miles. The main rivers are the Ganga, called the Padma in the region; the Jamuna called the Brahmaputra here, and the Meghna. The land is heavily flooded during the monsoon and takes several weeks to dry out. Vehicular movement off the main roads is very difficult and cross-country movement almost impossible.

Understandably this land, with its huge rivers, swamps, mangroves and paddy fields, and sparse roads and railways is very easy to defend. The very few bridges across the rivers add to the difficulties of the enemy. Crossing is feasible only by ferry. Conversely, a military assault in such terrain is a formidable task, as not only troops but ammunition, stores and supplies must be transported across one river after another. Fortunately for us, the Pakistanis had concentrated their troops in the towns. Had they chosen to defend approaches to the river crossing sites, we would

55

not have been able to cross the river and reach Dacca.

The alignment of the rivers divides the land into four sectors. North of the river Ganga or Padma and west of the river Brahmaputra lies the north-western sector, the main towns being Dinajpur, Rangpur, Bogra and Rajshahi. It is connected to the western sector by the Hardinge Railway Bridge across the Ganga. In the north it borders the narrow Siliguri corridor through which pass vital road and railway communications to the whole of north-eastern India.

The western sector lies south and west of the Padma. The main towns are Jessore, Faridpur, Kushtia and the river port of Khulna. The south-eastern sector is the area lying east of the river Meghna, the main towns in this sector being Sylhet, Comilla and Chittagong, the main port in East Pakistan. The area east of the Brahmaputra and west of the Meghna comprises the north-eastern sector. The main towns/cities are Dacca, the capital, and Mymensingh.

It was my assessment that the Pakistani Army would try to defend all their territory. They would almost certainly defend the main towns and cities, assessing that the Indian aim would be to seize a sizable portion of territory in order to set up a credible Bangladesh Government-in-exile. This assessment was confirmed fairly early on, when, the Pakistanis started fortifying the road approaches to these towns and later, the towns themselves.

I had no doubt that Dacca was the geopolitical and geostrategic heart of East Pakistan and that the capture of Dacca was the essential part of any operation. As far as the other sectors were concerned, I felt that capturing towns would be time consuming and would result in heavy casualties. If we could seize critical communication centres we would be able to disrupt the Pakistani defence posture and force a retreat. In the north-west sector, because of its location, Bogra was the main communication centre and should be our key objective. It could be approached along the main road Hilli–Gaibanda but since this was the obvious approach it was likely to be well defended. There were other approaches but they also were obvious. Fortunately, later, when we were able to get up-to-date maps, we spotted a fair weather motorable road shown near Phulbari up to Pirganj, north of Bogra. Use of this approach would bypass Pakistani defences and open up the approach to Bogra from the north.

In the west, the main communication centre was Jessore from which there was a road to Faridpur, near the ferry site on the Padma for crossing to Dacca. En route there are the two communication centres of Jhenida and Magura. Jessore could be bypassed from the north and Faridpur used as a mounting site for an attack on Dacca across the river.

In the south-eastern sector, control of the Meghna from Chandpur to Ashuganj was essential, as Dacca would then be isolated from Chittagong and Comilla. Further, control of the area would facilitate operations for the capture of Dacca. The three key points were Chandpur, Daudkandi and Ashuganj. In the northern part of this sector, the main communication centre was Maulvi Bazar and the airfield at Shamshernagar. Sylhet could be easily isolated and there was no compelling need for its early capture. The capture of Chittagong also took low priority as with our naval superiority the port could be effectively blockaded. Moreover, it was located almost in the extreme east and far from the military centre of gravity.

Dacca, the geopolitical heart, was difficult to approach. The Brahmaputra, Padma and Meghna are several miles wide. To the north, the river Brahmaputra on Pakistani maps which flows into the Brahmaputra on Indian maps is also very wide. Dacca can also be approached from the north-west on the Bogra–Phulcharighat axis and then across the Brahmaputra. From the north the thrust should be along the Jamalpur–Tangail axis and thence to Dacca. Dacca could also be approached from the western sector on the Jhenida–Magura–Faridpur–Goalundo Ghat axis. The main obstacles would be the Madhumati river, and later the Padma. The approach from the south-west would mean crossing the Meghna and Lakhya rivers, both extremely wide.

Strategy

At the time of the Bangladesh war, no institution of the Indian Army taught or studied strategy. Our military institutions taught tactics at the unit, brigade and to some extent divisional level. Consequently, no realistic, overall estimate of war situations by the Army Headquarters was made. There was, in fact, no strategic or political definition of policy, nor an appropriate higher command organization to plan or direct the war. Political objectives were rarely spelt out clearly. As a result, planning at Service Headquarters lacked depth.

Given the international climate and the possibility of the United Nations Security Council imposing a cease fire, any campaign, to be meaningful and effective, had to be swift and of short duration. As Brigade Commander, and later Divisional Commander, I had trained my troops to move using subsidiary tracks as axes of advance. In the desert warfare manual that I prepared in 1969 for 12 Infantry Division in the Rajasthan desert, I had stressed that the primary objectives should be communication and command centres and that the approaches to these should be along subsidiary tracks so as to bypass the main centres of resistance. Once the objective had been secured, a road axis could be opened later.

Unfortunately, it was very difficult to persuade our commanders to accept new concepts. They had throughout the years been used to moving along metalled roads with their maintenance elements following behind. It took a great deal of effort to convince them that the axis of advance and the axis of maintenance need not necessarily be the same. If the force could be maintained for limited durations an axis of maintenance could be opened later. Unfortunately, initially, most of the commanders were not prepared to operate in this manner as they were apprehensive of their flanks and did not wish to take even calculated risks. Time and again, during the operations, this preoccupation with flanks and maintenance was to lead to changes of thrust lines back to metalled roads and along routes the enemy was able to predict.

By the end of May 1971 I had made a draft plan based on the following strategic outline:

(*a*) The final objective was to be Dacca, the geopolitical and geostrategic heart of East Pakistan.

(*b*) Thrust lines were to be selected to isolate and bypass Pakistani forces to reach the final objective.

(*c*) Subsidiary objectives were to be selected with the aim of securing communication centres and the destruction of the enemy's command and control capabilities. Fortified centres of resistance were to be bypassed and dealt with later.

(*d*) Preliminary operations were aimed at drawing out the Pakistani forces to the border, leaving key areas in the interior lightly defended.

Eastern Command's task, before the crackdown, was to ensure the territorial integrity of India against possible Chinese aggression. In addition, we had to contain the insurgencies in Nagaland, Manipur and the Mizo Hills. We also had a commitment to defend Bhutan in case of any Chinese ingress. Moreover, the Army was already involved in assisting the state government of West Bengal in dealing with the Naxalite insurgency. Therefore, the availability of troops for any possible operations in East Pakistan would be largely qualified by requirements for the foregoing operations. After assessing the minimum strengths to be committed to a holding action against the Chinese, reserves and units in depth could be considered for operations in East Pakistan. Though the Chinese posture was hostile and pro-Pakistan, we felt that the quantum of troops committed to the defence of the northern border could be reduced, particularly if operations were to be launched in the winter when most of the mountain passes in the Himalayas would be closed. A minimum of two divisions of XXXIII Corps in Sikkim, 17 and 27 Mountain, and 71 Mountain Brigade would be required for the Siliguri corridor and two divisions of IV Corps in the North-East Frontier, 2 and 5 Mountain Divisions. In a worst case scenario we might have to cater for some troops for contingencies in Bhutan. The 6 Mountain Division of five battalions was earmarked later by Army Headquarters for western Bhutan and 167 Mountain Brigade for eastern Bhutan. We would have to leave one of the 8 Mountain Division's Brigades for counter-insurgency duties in Nagaland and Manipur and two battalions that had been organized for counter-insurgency duties would have to remain in Mizoram.

From our own resources, therefore, we could make the following troops available: 8 Mountain Division of two infantry brigades from Nagaland, though this Division had no artillery; IV Corps could move its reserve 23 Mountain Division from Assam and XXXIII Corps could make available its 20 Mountain Division in north Bengal; we could also utilize 57 Mountain Division from the Mizo Hills. This Division, too did not have its complete artillery component. The 95 Mountain Brigade could also be made available. When we sounded out Army Headquarters, they indicated that we could count on being allotted 9 Infantry Division, 4 Mountain Division, 340 Mountain Brigade Group and a battalion group of 50 Parachute Brigade, which was Army

61

Headquarters reserve. We suggested allocation of troops to tasks as follows:

North-Western Sector

The 20 Mountain Division, commanded by Maj Gen Lachhman Singh, with under command 340 Mountain Brigade Group to capture Bogra. The 71 Mountain Brigade could be used as the situation developed. Exploitation should be up to the river Brahmaputra.

Western Sector

The 9 Infantry and 4 Mountain Division were to capture Jessore, Magura and then Faridpur and, if opportunity permitted, to move to Dacca using the Inland Waterways Flotilla. We needed to raise a corps headquarters to command this force.

South-Eastern Sector

For the south-eastern sector, it was decided to allot 23 Mountain Division, 8 Mountain, less one brigade, and 57 Mountain Division. We could use Headquarters IV Corps to command this force. The Corps Headquarters could leave behind a small element under its Chief of Staff in Assam to perform its other tasks. The Corps was to secure the area up to the Meghna to include Chandpur and Daudkandi. I had earlier asked the FOC-in-C, Eastern Naval Command, Vice-Adm Krishnan, whether we could use his landing craft to ferry troops across the Meghna. Krishnan and Cmdr Dabir, who had brought one of them to Calcutta in June, stated that landing craft, of Russian origin, were unsuitable due to their draught. The question of crossing the Meghna had to be shelved and we shifted our attention to the possibility of obtaining additional helicopters.

North-Eastern Sector

We wanted one division plus one brigade to move on the Jamalpur–Tangail–Dacca axis. The parachute battalion could be utilized to drop at Tangail. Since we did not have a division for this task we suggested that 6 Mountain Division be made up to strength, and an additional brigade be used for this. In all operations the support of Mukti Bahini forces was visualized. This draft outline plan, hand written for reasons of security, was discussed with the Director of Military Operations who had asked for it, in order to prepare the operation instruction of the Army Headquarters.

Meanwhile, I held a staff conference at Fort William and issued orders to build up the infrastructure and logistics based on the draft outline plan we had made, without waiting for the Army Headquarters operation instruction. Poor road and rail communications, particularly in Tripura, and a complete lack of any viable infrastructure meant that preparations would have to start early. There was a metre gauge line from Assam to Dharamnagar in Tripura which had a capacity of 30 wagons a day. This had to be increased. The road from the rail head at Dharamnagar to Agartala and beyond was in poor condition and unable to take sustained heavy traffic. We requested the Border Roads Organization to increase the capacity and turnaround on this section. We moved the Sub Area Headquarters from Assam to Tripura to organize the infrastructure. Orders were issued for the placement of one month's requirements of ammunition, stores and supplies to commence immediately for two divisions at Teliamura, one division at Dharamnagar, two divisions at Krishnanagar in West Bengal, one division at Raiganj to the north in West Bengal and one division plus at Tura in Meghalaya.

It should be appreciated that this anticipatory action was taken before any operation order from Army Headquarters was issued, and just before the commencement of the monsoon. Had we waited for the operation instruction to come in from Army Headquarters or for the monsoon to end, we would not have been in a position to launch a successful offensive when the war did break out. The administrative areas, once established, would have been extremely difficult to move. This was a calculated risk and I would have been taken to task in case instructions issued by Army Head-quarters were incompatible with the administrative layout envisaged. Brig Chajju Ram, the Brigadier in charge of administration, worked with great dedication to have the administrative infrastructure built up. The Chief Signal Officer worked to establish telephone lines and microwave com-munications; the Chief Engineer, the road and rail communications, and to provide for the requirements of bridging and engineer stores. The services, such as the Ordnance Corps, Army Service Corps and the Army Medical Corps started obtaining and moving stores and ammunition. Work also started on building an air strip at Teliamura.

Chajju Ram came to me with some papers requiring the Army Commander's signature. As I was busy I told him to go directly to the Army Commander. When Aurora heard of the progress of the administrative build-up, he told Chajju Ram to suspend work until proper operational orders had arrived. It took some persuading to get Aurora to agree to let the build-up continue as he felt we should wait for the Army Head-quarters operation instruction. I had not been able to brief him earlier on the administrative moves as he was involved in advising the Mukti Bahini and spent much time touring. Since Sam Manekshaw insisted on daily reports from the Mukti Bahini about the buildup and training of the Mukti forces, I was left to get on with the planning, both opera-tional and logistic, for the regular Army.

Maj Gen Krishna Rao of the 8 Mountain Division visited me while he was transiting through Calcutta. I briefed him on his future role, concentration areas and the timeframe. He was surprised as Aurora, whom he had just met, had not mentioned a word about all this. He asked me to ensure that he would get two months for training as his Division was involved in counter-insurgency in Nagaland. I agreed. The 8 Mountain Division was suitably disengaged later and given the opportunity to train for their tasks which they later carried out with credit.

Eastern Command had Inland Waterways Flotillas located at Calcutta and on the Brahmaputra in Assam. The Calcutta Flotilla had river landing craft, some capable of carrying medium tanks. Since Vice-Adm Krishnan had declared his inability to operate landing craft in the Meghna, I asked the officer commanding the Inland Waterways Flotilla in Calcutta to see if it was possible to move to the Meghna. He tried the sea around the Sunderbans but found that the craft did not have sufficient free board. I then told him to be prepared to move to Farakka with a view to moving down the Ganga via the Hardinge Bridge to Faridpur in order to ferry troops across the river to Dacca at the onset of hostilities. We required lift for one brigade at a time. When he said he would have to hire more craft I told him to go ahead. This he did at Calcutta and Patna. He suggested that due to depth of the water in the river Hoogly, which he needed to reach Farakka, the move should take place in June–July as after the monsoon the river depths may not be adequate. I told him to plan the move for June and this he did. The Brahmaputra Flotilla was ordered to move to Dubri on the border by 15 November.

At the beginning of August Gen Manekshaw, accompanied by the Director of Military Operations Maj Gen K K Singh, came to Fort William to discuss the draft operation instruction sent to us a few days earlier. Though much of what we had sent had been incorporated into the draft, such as sectors and to some extent troop allocations, the essentials of the basic strategy and objectives had been left out. The aim as contained in the Army Headquarters operation instruction was to take as much territory as possible, with Khulna and Chittagong as prime objectives. Dacca was not even mentioned. This implied liberating large enough areas for setting up a free Bangladesh Government.

At the meeting, held in the operations room, Manekshaw, K K Singh, Aurora and I were present. Sam Manekshaw let his DMO do the talking. K K Singh spelt out the objectives, maintaining that if we captured Khulna and Chittagong, what he termed the entry ports, the war would come to an end. Further, Khulna was the key and the weight of our main attack should be directed at Khulna. The Hardinge Bridge was also to be secured. Both Manekshaw and Aurora nodded approvingly but I was flabbergasted. I got up to explain that in the event of hostilities, we should utilize our naval superiority and have an effective blockade in place. Next, Khulna was only a minor port; the main anchorage lay several miles downstream, at Mangla/Chalna. Cargoes for Khulna were off-loaded into light river craft for transportation to Khulna. There were several tidal rivers, unbridged, between our border and Khulna. The terrain restricted manoeuver as, intersected by several subsidiary water channels, it narrowed down considerably. As far as Chittagong was concerned, it was well east of the main centre of gravity, almost peripheral.

I maintained that the geopolitical heart of East Pakistan was Dacca and that if we wanted to ensure control of East Pakistan it was imperative that we capture Dacca. At this stage Gen Manekshaw intervened saying, 'Sweetie' (an expression he used to precede a mild or harsh rebuke), 'don't you see that if we take Khulna and Chittagong, Dacca will automatically fall?' I said I did not and reiterated that Dacca should be the key objective. There were further exchanges between the DMO and myself. Dacca, both Manekshaw and Singh maintained, was not a priority and no

66

troops were being allotted for its capture. Manekshaw then turned to Aurora and said, 'Jagjit don't you agree that if we take Khulna and Chittagong, Dacca will fall', to which Aurora replied, 'Yes Sir I entirely agree.' This was a view Aurora maintained until 30 November. I could not believe what I was hearing. Eventually Sam Manekshaw said he was prepared to make one change, namely that he would delete the word 'weight' in connection with the main thrust to Khulna. The meeting then ended.

In the planning period and during the operations, Manekshaw for the most part bypassed Aurora and dealt directly with the Chief of Staff, except for matters pertaining to the Mukti Bahini.

Outline plans based on the Army Headquarters operation instruction were sent to formations and studied by them. Detailed planning then began. We ordered war games to be held. The Army Commander and I attended these games at XXXIII Corps and II Corps after its raising. Unfortunately, I was not able to attend the war games of IV Corps as it would have entailed being absent from the Command Headquarters for two to three days. One had to take a long circuitous route around East Pakistan to reach IV Corps Headquarters.

In the war games held at XXXIII Corps the original concept of capturing Rangpur and Dinajpur was dropped as also the idea of advancing on the Hilli–Gaibanda axis. Our strategy was to bypass and get to the final objective, Bogra. I carried with me the Pakistani maps of the area that had been reproduced by the Survey of India. These maps showed an unmetalled road along the Phulbari–Nawabganj–Pirganj axis going south to Bogra. A thrust along this line would bypass the heavily fortified Hilli–Gaibanda approach. Much discussion took place, with the Corps Commander Lt Gen M L Thapan readily accepting my suggestion, but Aurora was still in favour of taking Rangpur. He had commanded XXXIII Corps before coming to Eastern Command and was of the opinion that Rangpur was the key objective. Thapan also opposed capturing Hilli as along its approaches heavily fortified concrete bunkers had been constructed. Later, when the preliminary operations began, he opposed our troops and the Mukti Bahini attacking Hilli, but was overruled by Aurora, as Gen Manekshaw was keen on capturing it.

The war game at II Corps led to acrimonious exchanges. The thrust line we had selected for 4 Mountain Division was Shikarpur–Kushtia–Jhenida, to link up with the thrust line Darsana–Kotchandpur–Jhenida. This thrust would have facilitated the capture of the Hardinge Bridge, an objective specified by Army Headquarters. We selected the thrust line Bayra–Jessore for 9 Infantry Divsion. The GOC, Maj Gen Dalbir Singh, preferred to move along the axis of the main Bangaon–Jessore road. The Corps Commander Lt Gen 'Tappy' Raina, however, opposed the concept of the northern thrust line as he was, as he put it, worried about his flank. He wanted 4 Mountain Division to move on an axis in close proximity to 9 Infantry Division. It has always appeared strange to me that in the preliminary operations carried out by the Corps in conjunction with the Mukti Bahini, the surprise element on the proposed Shikarpur–Jhenida axis was compromised by undertaking border incursions there. Naik Joshi and three others of the Naga Regiment were captured at Shikarpur and paraded in Dacca before the international press. A preliminary operation was also carried out at Bayra by 9 Infantry Division, which had many repercussions which will be apparent later. Both these preliminary operations appeared to me to be designed to ensure that II Corps would move its 4 and 9 Divisions in close proximity to each other, as desired by Raina.

I was unable to attend the IV Corps war games but had a discussion with the Army Commander regarding Lt Gen Sagat Singh's plan to capture Comilla, Maynamati Cantonment and the dominating Lalmai heights. Air photos showed considerable fortification works in hand. Due to 23 Mountain Division's preliminary operations in the Belonia area and the improvement of road communications in the area, we felt 23 Mountain Division was now suitably poised to advance on the Chaudagram–Laksham–Chandpur axis. The plan then agreed upon was to contain Comilla with one brigade of 57 Mountain Division, after which 57 Mountain Division, less a brigade, would swing south to Daudkandi.

The 8 Mountain Division of two brigades commanded by Maj Gen Krishna Rao would capture Shamshernagar and Maulvi Bazar, after which it would contain Sylhet with one brigade. The other brigade of 8 Mountain Division was to be grouped as Corps reserve.

No war game was held for the 101 Communication Zone as other than the 95 Mountain Brigade, troops had yet to be allotted. However, the GOC was thoroughly briefed by me. The essentials of the plan have already been indicated. The GOC was enthusiastic and felt he could reach the outskirts of Dacca in under ten days.

Throughout history the conduct of military operations has been shaped to a considerable degree by the personalities of commanders and their staff, as also the relationship between them. Manekshaw's handling of senior officers was not conducive to creating confidence. A typical example of this was when he decided, in late September, to address all formation commanders of the rank of Major General and above in the operations room of Eastern Command. He berated the efforts of all formations, and made no attempt to hide his displeasure at their performance. He behaved like a headmaster scolding his senior form. His criticisms were largely unwarranted as Manekshaw, in Delhi, had little feel of the situation on the ground. The commanders did not appreciate the presence of D P Dhar, who had accompanied Manekshaw and witnessed the proceedings. Dhar was the Prime Minister's advisor for Bangladesh and close to her.

Formation commanders were looking to Aurora to speak up for them, but he was apologetic in his answers to Manekshaw. When I tried to intercede Manekshaw cut me short telling me to let Aurora speak. Aurora, who was completely overawed by Manekshaw, remained silent. The berating continued. The effect of this 'pep' talk turned out to be counter-productive and was deeply resented by formation commanders who were doing their best to produce results. It further strained relations between some formation commanders and the Army Commander, as they had expected some support from him. Loyalty is a two way street—both up and down.

Friction also developed between Thapan and Aurora and their relationship was strained almost to breaking point. Thapan was not only an upright man but also a competent commander who took his profession seriously. Their relationship worsened regarding the naming of a cinema after Aurora at the Corps Headquarters. In those days it was not customary to name institutions after serving officers, but Aurora considered Thapan's stance to be a personal affront. Relations between Sagat Singh and Aurora also, initially cordial, soon deteriorated as Sagat felt that Aurora was not backing him against Manekshaw's criticism of his performance. Aurora got on well with Raina but in the case of G S Gill bent to Manekshaw's tirades, thereby straining his relations with this competent officer.

Relations between the corps commanders and their divisional commanders were for the most part cordial. However, in the case of II Corps, Lt Gen Raina had little control over Maj Gen Dalbir Singh who paid scant heed to what Raina had to say. This was to have an adverse effect on the conduct of II Corps operations. Sagat Singh had problems later both with Maj Gen B F Gonsalves of 57 Mountain Division and R D Hira of 23 Mountain Division.

THE TAKE-OFF FOR FULL-SCALE WAR

Due to shelling of our border posts by Pakistan, it was decided in November to allow our troops to go into East Pakistan up to a depth of ten miles to silence these guns. We took advantage of these instructions to secure specific areas to improve our offensive posture. Initially we instructed formations to carry out the following tasks, expanding them as the situations developed.

II Corps: Invest enemy defences in area Afra and capture Mohammadpur. Secure the Khalispur Bridge and capture Uthali. No tasks were given by Command Headquarters for Bayra and Shikarpur.

XXXIII Corps: Clear Pachagarh and advance as far south as possible towards Thakurgaon. Capture Hilli.

The 101 Communication Zone Area: Capture Jaintiapur. Capture Kamalpur and advance to Bakshiganj. Intensify Mukti Bahini activity in Tangail and threaten Mymensingh, Haluaghat, Phulpur, Shamganj and Durgapur.

IV Corps: Capture Gangasagar and clear area up to Saidabad. Establish a battalion block in area Debigram. Isolate Akhaura and Brahman Baria. Eliminate Pakistani border posts in Narayanpur area. Capture Rajpur and threaten Akhaura. Secure Shamshernagar and Kalhura. Isolate Feni.

Consequently, at the commencement of hostilities our posture was as follows:

WESTERN SECTOR

Chaugacha was firmly in our hands by 29 November, thanks to the Mukti Bahini. The 9 Infantry Division had reached Arpana which was almost halfway between the border and

Jessore on the Chaugacha–Jessore axis. A bridge had been constructed across the Bhairab river at Bayra and the road to Chaugacha had been linked from Bayra. On 24 November Mrs Gandhi had announced in Parliament the shooting down of three Pakistani Sabre jets in Bayra sector. This interception had, in fact, been controlled from Fort William in liaison with the formation at Bayra.

The 4 Mountain Division had captured Jibannagar, Uthali, Darsana and advanced towards Khalispur on the Jibannagar–Kotchandpur axis and up to Silinda on the Darsana–Kotchandpur axis.

North-Western Sector

Parts of the Hilli defences like Naoara, Monapara and Basudebpur had been occupied but the Pakistanis continued to resist at Hilli itself. In the area of Dinajpur, Khanpur and Mukunalpur had been occupied. On the Samja–Phulbari axis both banks of the Ichamati river were secured.

The 71 Mountain Brigade advancing on the Morgarh–Dinajpur axis had captured Thakurgaon.

Barakhatta had been captured. In the Nagheshwar salient all the area north of the Dharla river had been cleared.

South-Eastern Sector

In the Karimganj area the salient east of the line Chargam–Karimganj had been secured.

In the area of Kalaura, Ghazipur had been captured and Kalaura invested. Shamshernagar airfield was in our hands.

In the Akhaura area Gangasagar had been captured. A block had been established west of Akhaura. Further south the whole of the Belonia bulge had been cleared.

In these preliminary operations whenever we attacked the

Pakistanis in their prepared defences, they fought with courage and doggedness. In the attacks on the Hilli defences which commenced on orders from Manekshaw which were conveyed by Aurora on 23 November, we suffered 67 killed and 90 wounded. Hilli was finally cleared on 11 December. In the north-eastern sector, Kamalpur could not be captured inspite of two attacks by 95 Mountain Brigade. The garrison surrendered only after their supplies ran out. The Teliakhali post was captured at the cost of 23 killed and 35 wounded. In the south-eastern sector the Khalai post, initially held by one Pakistani platoon (later reinforced to two companies), repulsed two consecutive attacks and was finally cleared by a whole brigade. On 20 November 9 Infantry Division launched a preliminary operation in the area of Bayra. The Pakistan Air Force reacted but ended up losing three of its aircraft. Our Infantry was supported by tanks which had taken up hull down positions. I happened to be visiting the troops and through binoculars I saw an officer, who appeared to be Niazi, in his jeep lining up a squadron of Chaffee tanks. Then taking a leaf out of the Earl of Cardigan's Light Brigade, the squadron charged over open ground to be met by concentrated tank and recoilless gun fire. In this battle at Bayra the Pakistanis lost 14 tanks, 3 aircraft and a large number of men.

These preliminary operations reinforced Eastern Command's strategic concept that fortified positions had to be bypassed as they took a long time and great cost to reduce.

The Pakistanis were thrown off balance and our strategy of drawing the Pakistanis to the border began to work. We secured suitable jumping off places, particularly where obstacles had to be crossed, and such operations also gave our troops realistic initiation into battle.

The Pakistani deployment was designed to defend territory

and deny any attempts at the establishment of a free Bangladesh Government. Niazi concentrated on the defence of Jessore, Jhenida, Bogra, Rangpur, Mymensingh, Sylhet, Bhairab Bazar, Comilla and Chittagong and ordered these towns to be turned into fortresses. Other important towns were to be turned into strong points. We had anticipated this policy as also the fortification of the main approaches to these fortified towns. Niazi's strategy, as we had correctly assessed, was that troops deployed on the border should fight on until ordered to withdraw, delaying our advance as they withdrew into the fortresses which would be defended to the last. This strategy left open subsidiary axes which we proposed to use.

The Army Headquarters operation instruction (based on the draft discussed at Fort William) was issued on 16 August. Based on this instruction additional moves and deployments were ordered with provisional objectives and thrust lines. Confirmatory orders based on the war games were to be issued later.

NORTH-WESTERN SECTOR

The 20 Mountain Division under Maj Gen Lachhman Singh, with the command of 340 Mountain Brigade Group was originally to secure the Hilli–Gaibanda axis and thereafter capture Bogra. Exploitation was to be up to the river Brahmaputra. The main thrust line was changed in October/ November when the Pakistani maps of this area came into our hands showing a motorable track to Pirganj. The thrust line later given was eastwards via Phulbari, Nawabganj and Pirganj and thence south to Gobindganj and Bogra, thus bypassing the defences at Hilli–Gaibanda. The axis of maintenance was to be opened later. The 71 Mountain Brigade from the north was to capture Thakurgaon and threaten Dinajpur–Saidpur. Dinajpur was to be contained by para-military forces. Elements of 6 Mountain Division under

Maj Gen Reddy, which were standing by for the defence of
Bhutan, were to simulate a threat towards Rangpur by
capturing the area north of the Teesta, but remain in a state
of readiness to move to Bhutan as and when required by
Army Headquarters. The Inland Waterways Flotilla in Assam
was moved to Dubri on the border to assist 20 Division, if
necessary, as well as the troops moving to Dacca on the
Jamalpur–Tangail axis.

WESTERN SECTOR

Army Headquarters sanctioned the raising of II Corps
Headquarters on 31 October 1971, on a reduced static
establishment which meant that it had very little transport
and was incapable of moving once established. Personnel
started arriving in November. Until the Headquarters was
formed, Eastern Command Headquarters organized its
communications and infrastructure. The II Corps, commanded by Lt Gen T N Raina, was allotted 9 Infantry Division
under Maj Gen Dalbir Singh, and 4 Mountain Division under
Maj Gen Barar. The 9 Infantry Division was to capture Jessore
and to assist 4 Mountain Division to capture Magura. One of
its brigades was to capture Khulna later. The 4 Mountain
Division was to capture Jhenida, Magura, Faridpur and
Goalundo Ghat. A small force was to secure the Hardinge
Bridge. Contingency plans were drawn for elements of II
Corps to cross the Brahmaputra at Goalundo Ghat. For this
purpose the Inland Waterways Flotilla was moved from
Calcutta to Farakka in June–July in order to facilitate its
movement down the river to Faridpur and later to Dacca, if
so required.

SOUTH-EASTERN SECTOR

The IV Corps, under Lt Gen Sagat Singh, consisted of
8 Mountain Division less one brigade under Maj Gen Krishna
Rao; 23 Mountain Division under Maj Gen R D Hira and

57 Mountain Division under Maj Gen B F Gonsalves. The 57 Mountain Division was to contain Comilla and the rest of the Division was to proceed to Daudkandi. Information at this stage indicated that the terrain near Brahman Baria and Ashuganj was unfavourable; further, approaches to the Coronation Bridge over the Meghna were defended by an infantry brigade.

The 23 Mountain Division was to advance to Chandpur, bypassing Comilla. The 8 Mountain Division of two brigades was to secure Shamshernagar–Maulvi Bazar with one brigade, and contain or, if possible, take Sylhet. One brigade of the Division was to be Corps reserve to be used only with the approval of Command Headquarters. There was one infantry battalion of 101 Communication Zone Area of Shillong. This battalion was to assist 8 Mountain Division in operations against Sylhet by posing a threat from Dauki in the north. The IV Corps was also to pose a threat to Dacca. For this purpose they were allotted the complete Mi4 helicopter resources, i.e. fourteen helicopters. These were sent to them prior to operations for training. We were also promised two squadrons of Mi8 helicopters. These were to be allotted to IV Corps for operations across the Meghna. These helicopters, unfortunately, did not arrive at all. Perhaps if they had, IV Corps would have made an effective rather than a token crossing of the Meghna.

NORTH-EASTERN SECTOR

Army Headquarters allotted no troops for Dacca as it did not consider its capture to be of importance, and had not spelt it out as an objective. Despite repeated requests to Manekshaw to allot 6 Mountain Division, no action was taken. We had to find the troops and the controlling Headquarters. We asked to use Headquarters 2 Mountain Division from eastern Assam. This too was turned down. We had no option but to use Headquarters 101 Communication Zone commanded by Maj Gen Gurbax Singh Gill, an officer of high calibre. We discussed the capture of Dacca and Gurbax Gill wanted at least a division for the task. We made up 95 Mountain Brigade into a brigade group of four battalions with supporting artillery. We planned an airdrop of one battalion group from 50 Parachute Brigade which was to drop at Tangail. This was the area, on the road to Dacca, controlled by 'Tiger' Siddiqui reportedly leading 20,000 Mukti Bahini. Also available was one battalion of the Bihar Regiment under Brig Sant Singh. We had to find two more brigades. These we intended to move down from the Himalaya closer to the expected time of hostilities. The plan, therefore, was to cross the Brahmaputra at Jamalpur, hopefully with three or four brigades, and link up with the Parachute Battalion at Tangail. The combined force was to advance to Dacca together with Siddiqui's forces. In October, the Senior Air Staff officer, Eastern Air Command, Air Vice Marshal Devashar, the Commander 50 Parachute Brigade, Brig Mathew Thomas and I prepared the operation instruction for the air drop. It is for the record that even at that early date we spelt out that the para drop would occur on D plus 7 and the link up within twenty-four hours. Subsequent events were to prove the accuracy of this time frame.

Prior to the para drop we sent an advance party with signal detachment under Capt P. K. Ghosh of 50 Para Brigade to Tangail to liaise with Siddiqui for the preparation of a dropping zone for 2 Para Battalion group's air drop. Ghosh also briefed Siddiqui and asked for his assistance in the collection of stores that were to be dropped as also in establishing a road block. Siddiqui was also told that in the event of war his forces were to move with our troops to Dacca. After the outbreak of war he assisted in the para drop but took no offensive action against withdrawing Pakistani troops. He did, however, move part of his force to Dacca after the cease fire.

Logistics

The critical factor throughout was logistics. The success of the coming campaign would depend on our ability to equip the troops adequately, move them to their concentration areas and create administrative complexes with the infrastructure to sustain them. This was to be done in areas with inadequate road and rail communications and without any supporting infrastructure. Roads had to be built, depots constructed, accommodation fabricated, ammunition moved, stores and rations procured and moved. Logistics was the critical factor throughout.

One of the major problems we faced was bridging. Although we had worked out the quantum of bridging required based on the draft outline plan and sent our requirements to Army Headquarters in June, no physical movement of bridging took place until mid-August. The bridging we got was nearly all of World War II vintage: Bailey pontoon and folding boat equipment from the numerous depots spread throughout India. The modern, serviceable bridging equipment was kept in reserve for the Western Theatre, where it remained unutilized. A little over half the folding boats were in position at the commencement of operations. Assault boats arrived late and were in position only a few days before commencement of hostilities. Most of the equipment needed major repairs and it was we who had to arrange for the repairs. The bridging was repaired in time. The dedicated efforts of the Chief Engineer and his staff, however, saw to it that it was ready by the time we needed it.

The greatest difficulty was experienced in the movement of stores to the corps maintenance areas. It was fortunate that movement started in July and we were just able to complete it before operations commenced. The jumping off points for the three corps were in areas not previously used for troop concentrations. Of these Tripura proved the most difficult. Corps dumps were established at Teliamura, Udaipur and Dharamnagar. Some 30,000 tons of stores were moved to their locations in Tripura for IV Corps; 14,000 tons to Krishnanagar for II Corps; 7,000 tons to Raigarh for XXXIII Corps and 4,000 tons to Tura for the thrust to Dacca.

Field hospitals were established at Dharamnagar, Teliamura and Silchar. In Tripura a new road network was created to cater for dumps and jumping off points for which two Task Forces of the General Reserve of Engineer Forces (GREF) were utilized. For 23 Mountain Division's operations 45 kilometres of new roads had to be constructed and the capacity of the metre gauge railway was more than doubled.

Signal communications in our theatre of operations were highly underdeveloped paricularly in Tripura and Meghalaya. The existing post and telegraph network could barely cater to civilian requirements; for our purpose it was grossly inadequate. We had to create a new signal communications infrastructure for IV Corps and its earmarked divisions, though they had not yet moved to Tripura. Similarly, II Corps Headquarters, yet to be raised at Krishnanagar, had to be provided with signal communications together with its two divisions. Communications for a divisional headquarters were established at Tura in Meghalaya and also at Cooch Behar. New military telephonic exchanges were procured and installed at Fort William, Shillong, Krishnanagar, Tura, Teliamura and Dharamnagar. We were to rely heavily on electronic teleprinter circuits, which were linked to Army

Headquarters and formations, and they proved to be reliable and secure.

We were short of vehicles. The mountain divisions were organized on very restricted scales of transport. Besides making up transport scales for mountain divisions to operate in the plains, we required transport to move the vast tonnage of stores required to stock the various maintenance areas. Army Headquarters, though unable to provide us any transport vehicles, offered us a hundred chassis. Apparently, they did not have the capacity to have the vehicle bodies built. We had these chassis driven to the vehicle depot at Panagarh, which was holding a large numbers of old vehicles for disposal. During September–October 1971 we had the old vehicle bodies removed and fitted onto these chassis. They did not look smart, but served our purpose. We sent teams out as far afield as central India to hire over two thousand civilian load carriers.

There were chronic shortages of weapons and equipment, particularly medium machine guns, light machine guns and recoilless anti-tank guns. Persistent efforts were made to order the equipment from depots to make up these deficiencies. The spares position for small arms was equally disturbing. We had to approach local factories in and around Calcutta to manufacture breach blocks for light machine guns and firing pins. Provisioning of tank tracks and links for our amphibious PT 76 tanks caused considerable anxiety. These arrived at Bombay port only in the third week of November and were flown to Calcutta, courtesy Indian Airlines. There was also a shortage of dry batteries for the radio sets. The Master General of Ordnance at Army Headquarters declared his inability to provision these due to constraints of shelf life, in case there was no war and they were not needed later. Brig Sethna approached his friends in the trade and they commenced manufacture in August–September 1971. Some of these were later transferred to the Master General of

Ordnance, at his request, for other theatres.

The divisional artillery in Eastern Command consisted almost entirely of mountain guns. The 4 and 23 Mountain Divisions had 76 mm Yugoslav howitzers and a pack light regiment equipped with 120 mm mortars—the Israeli Tampella in the case of 4 Mountain Division and Brandt in the case of 23 Mountain Division. The ammunition for these mortars was not interchangeable. The 20 Mountain Division had three regiments of 75/24 howitzers and one regiment of 120 mm Brandt mortars. The 57 Mountain Division had, on reduced establishment, one regiment of 75/24 howitzers and the other of 3.7 inch howitzers. The 8 Mountain Division, which initially had six brigades in Nagaland, had no artillery whatsoever. There were in the Command only two medium regiments of 5.5 inch howitzers and these were deployed on our northern border. The air observation resources consisted of two flights equipped with Allouette helicopters and two fixed wing flights of Krishak aircraft. To provide more resources six Pushpak aircraft were hired from flying clubs. The weight of fire that could be generated was very limited— the 75 mm howitzer fired a 13 pound shell with limited destructive effect.

The provisioning of ammunition and spares was also an enormous problem due to the numerous types involved. In the month of July we decided to reorganize and rationalize the artillery headquarters and regiments. We moved Headquarters 2 Artillery Brigade from the northern border and allotted it to the newly raised II Corps as the Corps Artillery Brigade Headquarters, because it had not been allotted any artillery headquarters. We also tried to let each division have the same type of gun. We converted pack units to towed units and as far as possible we made up deficiencies of formations by moving down artillery units from the northern border. In moving down the two medium artillery regiments, leaving only a token force, behind we took a calculated risk. Later, Army Headquarters allotted one regiment of 5.5 inch howitzers and one of 130 mm guns. They also allotted two locating batteries for detecting mortars. The School of Artillery sent us some personnel and equipment for locating guns. In November we received 12 single barrel rocket launchers (Grad P), and two rocket batteries were immediately formed, one allotted to 23 Mountain Division and one to 9 Infantry Division. The 23 Mountain Division used their rocket batteries to great effect but 9 Infantry Division could not employ them as no rockets were available.

The calculated risks we took in thinning out the artillery units on our northern border and the reorganization and rationalization of the various types of artillery with each division, thus simplifying the provision of ammunition, spares and workshop cover was done on our own initiative, without reference to Army Headquarters. Thus, when hostilities did commence the artillery support provided was adequate, despite constraints of the lightweight shell of the 75 mm howitzers.

Orders for raising Headquarters II Corps having been issued on 31 October, personnel started arriving in November. Headquarters Eastern Command had established the infrastructure, communications and maintenance areas in anticipation of events so that the Corps Headquarters was able to function almost immediately after induction of personnel.

The air defence component consisted of six regular light anti-aircraft regiments and three territorial. Considering the limited threat and our own air power superiority, these were more than adequate.

Perhaps the greatest achievement of the 1971 war was the foresight shown in setting up a viable infrastructure, and providing communications and logistical cover for operations. Work had commenced before any operation order was issued. It was a great logistical achievement on the part of the administrative staff at command, corps, area, sub area and the various divisional headquarters. The Engineers, Signals, Electrical and Mechanical Engineers, Workshops, Supply Organizations of the Army Service Corps, Ordnance, Medical and Postal Services of Command worked with dedication. When hostilities did commence our troops did not have to look back. Almost everything had been catered for. This was an outstanding achievement and due credit should be given to all those who made it possible, particularly the Brigadier General Staff, Adi Sethna, the Brigadier incharge of Administration, Chajju Ram and the Chief Engineer Brig Baba Bhide.

Pakistani Order of Battle

Let us now consider the Pakistani order of battle at the commencement of hostilities. (For a detailed order of battle and deployment see Appendix 7 and the pull-out map.)

North-Western Sector

The 16 Infantry Division under Maj Gen Nazar Hussain Shaker with headquarters at Nator had a reconnaissance and support battalion, a regiment less a squadron of armour, two field regiments of artillery and one heavy mortar battery. The Division deployed 23 Infantry Brigade of four battalions in the area Dinajpur–Rangpur, 205 Infantry Brigade in the area Hilli–Ghoraghat and 34 Infantry Brigade in the area Rajshahi–Naogaon. This was the most heavily defended sector and one of its tasks was the cutting off of the Siliguri corridor.

Western Sector

The 9 Infantry Division under Maj Gen M H Ansari had a squadron of armour, two field regiments and one mortar battery. Divisional Headquarters, together with 107 Infantry Brigade, was located in the Jessore area and 57 Infantry Brigade in Jhenida–Meherpur–Jibannagar. There were also some elements at Satkhira. Pakistani deception postures were designed to indicate a larger quantum of troops in this area and in this they were partially successful, I failed to see

84

through their stimulated signal traffic and over estimated the troop deployment in this sector.

South-Eastern Sector

The 14 Infantry Division under Maj Gen Abdul Majid Quazi, with a squadron of armour, two field regiments and one heavy mortar battery was deployed in the northern part of this sector. The Headquarters was initially at Dacca but later moved to Bhairab Bazar. The 17 Infantry Brigade was in the area Akhaura–Kasba–Brahman Baria, 313 Infantry Brigade at Maulvi Bazar and 202 Infantry Brigade at Sylhet. The 39 Infantry Division, commanded by Maj Gen Rual Rahim Khan, was in the southern part of this sector, its headquarters at Chandpur. The 117 Infantry Brigade was in the Maynamati area and 53 Infantry Brigade of two battalions in the area of Feni. The 91 Infantry Brigade of one regular infantry battalion together with a para military force was at Faujdahat–Ramgarh. The 91 Infantry Brigade was deployed in the area of Chittagong, with some elements in the Chittagong hill tracts.

North-Eastern Sector

Headquarters 36 Infantry Division was formed from the Director General of East Pakistan's Civil Armed Forces. It had under its command 93 Infantry Brigade together with one battery deployed in the area Jamalpur–Mymensingh. One brigade's worth of troops were located at Dacca.

In addition to these regular troops, each division was given large numbers of East Pakistan Civil Armed Police (EPCAP) Mujahids and Razakars, operating together with regular Army personnel.

Preparatory Moves
and Training

At the beginning of October, preparatory moves of formations started in accordance with the outline tasks given to them. Regrouping was carried out and a large number of formations and units were raised. Only XXXIII Corps Headquarters in north Bengal was able to control offensive operations from its location. The II Corps Headquarters, on a reduced static establishment, had yet to be raised at Krishnanagar. The IV Corps Headquarters was split, leaving behind a rear element under Chief of Staff Maj Gen O P Malhotra to look after the northern border.

It was important that realistic training be given on the type of terrain on which formations and units would be fighting. Due to large scale regrouping of units it was necessary for these to train together. Further, we had a pretty good idea by now of Pakistani tactics and techniques employed against the liberation forces. We had also noted the construction of defences around the main towns and the approaches to them. We trained units to bypass the main centres of resistance and to use subsidiary approaches: movement was to be the key to the conduct of successful operations.

New equipment was also being inducted, such as wheeled armoured personnel carriers. We selected two infantry battalions to be reorganized as mechanized infantry. A crash training programme was undertaken. I drew up the establishment tables and produced the tactical doctrines and operating procedures for these two battalions of mechanized infantry. For the first time in India mechanized infantry units were to be employed in operations. The months of October and November were devoted to intensive training including air–land operations. Helicopters were placed at the disposal of IV Corps to train for the coming operations. On 14 October 1971 all the Border Security Force battalions located in Eastern Command were placed under our operational control. Prior to this only the battalions on the border were so designated.

By September the operations of the Mukti Bahini were beginning to have an effect on the morale of the Pakistani Army. Raids and ambushes were carried out, culverts and bridges blown up. The Pakistani Army's will to fight, particularly of the rank and file, was being greatly eroded. As the raids led to reprisals, Pakistani artillery started shelling the Mukti Bahini. Some of our border posts in the process came under Pakistani artillery fire. In view of these developments, we were officially authorized to occupy areas across the border to prevent Pakistani shelling.

Our operation plans, spelt out to all formations in our preliminary orders, were based on the following strategy. We were to (*a*) draw enemy forces to the border and dissipate enemy reserves; (*b*) launch major thrusts at key communication centres, bypassing fortified defensive positions; (*c*) destroy the enemy's command and control network paralysing his forces; and (*d*) as opportunities arose, cross the Meghna and the Padma to supplement the main thrust from the north to Dacca.

There was very little we could do to change the weightage of troops that had been allotted to the three corps and in the general locations as spelt out by Army Headquarters in their operation instruction. However, we could, at our own risk, thin out troops from the northern border. This we had already started doing by moving artillery units and an artillery brigade headquarters. We had also utilized several infantry battalions. Since we could not get Army Headquarters to agree to designate Dacca as an objective and make troop allocations for its capture, and as Manekshaw would not permit the use of 6 Mountain Division which he kept in reserve for Bhutan, I told the Director of Military Operations, Inder Gill that we planned to move down, from the northern border, 123 Mountain Brigade, 167 Mountain Brigade earmarked for eastern Bhutan by Army Headquarters, and 5 Mountain Brigade. Inder, pragmatic as ever, approved of these moves. We required a Headquarters to command this force. In view of the non-availability of field headquarters we decided to utilize Headquarters 101 Communication Zone, suitably augmented. The GOC was a fine practical soldier with boundless energy. I had discussed with Maj Gen Gurbax Singh Gill the pattern of the operations. He asked for more troops; I told him that the parachute battalion group would be dropped at Tangail on D plus 7 and that he should be able to link up within twenty-four hours. The 95 Mountain Brigade Group with four battalions and supporting artillery was placed under his command. We would, in addition, allot 167 Mountain Brigade and 5 Mountain Brigade. He was briefed on the Inland Waterways Flotilla that was moved to Dubri on the Brahmaputra which could be used for ferrying and if necessary, moved later to Jamalpur. The Flotilla was placed under his command at his request. He was briefed on the river crossing equipment, including a large bridge to be moved to Tura. I suggested to him to also employ the Bihar Battalion allotted to Brig Sant Singh. There were reportedly 20,000 Mukti Bahini at Tangail under command of 'Tiger' Siddiqui. These were to be utilized for the protection of the dropping zone of the parachute battalion group and subsequently to advance with his forces to Dacca. We agreed on the time frame to contact Dacca. Gurbax Gill wanted the 167 and 5 Mountain Brigades put under his command immediately. I explained that this was not possible as at Army Headquarters only the Director of Military Operations was briefed on the projected move of these brigades. The Army Chief had yet to be convinced that the Chinese would not attack while we were busy fighting the Pakistanis. The essentials of our discussions were sent to him in a demi official letter (DO). It was unfortunate that Gurbax was injured during the operations, on 5 December, when his jeep ran into a landmine. Fortunately, he was able, later, to brief his relief at the hospital. In early November we issued order for the 123, 167 and 5 Mountain Brigades to move down to suitable concentration areas. I informed the Director of Military Operations of the move on the telephone.

Mukti Bahini

On the request of the Provisional Government of Bangladesh, the Government of India directed the Army to provide assistance to the Mukti Bahini who controlled areas of East Pakistan contiguous to our borders. The code name given to the guerrilla operations in East Pakistan was 'Operation Jackpot'. The recruitment and control operations of the Mukti Bahini was set up on a regional basis with their headquarters located at Calcutta at 'Mujibnagar' in Theatre Road. It was headed by Col M G Osmani, with Wing Cmdr Khondkar as his deputy. Maj Zia was to be responsible for the Chittagong sector, Maj Khalid Musharaf for Comilla, Maj Safiullah for Mymensingh, Wing Cmdr Bashar for Rangpur, Lt Col Zaman for Rajshahi, Maj Usman for Kushtia and Maj Jalil for Khulna. 'Tiger' Siddiqui elected to operate from his own area in Tangail as did Noorul Kadar and Toha. We had visualized training some 8,000 guerrillas in the border areas. Recruits were to be given three months training. An additional period of specialized training would be required for leaders. Once trained, these guerrillas would penetrate deep into East Pakistan to form cells and function in the manner that guerrilla forces throughout history have done. Osmani also required a very large number of recruits to make the existing East Bengal battalions upto strength as also to man the large number of additional East Bengal battalions and artillery batteries that he planned to raise. However, the

Provisional Government visualized the Mukti Bahini training a force of 100,000 and felt that three weeks of training would be adequate. We felt that in the period of some six or seven months the Mukti Bahini would find it difficult to put together an effective force of 100,000 guerrillas; that a figure of 8000 would be more realistic In addition several thousand recruits had also to be trained for the East Bengal battalions and artillery batteries. Maj Gen Onkar Singh Kalkat was then deputed by Manekshaw to work directly with Aurora who was given overall responsibility for assisting the Mukti Bahini for 'Operation Jackpot'. This left me free to organize the logistics and also plan operations. Manekshaw required daily updates on the progress of the training. Kalkat, a good, orthodox soldier found it difficult to cope with this assignment. We did our best to help him function in this unfamiliar environment. However, Onkar Kalkat was replaced barely two months later by Maj Gen B N (Jimmy) Sarcar. Aurora spent most of his time with Sarcar in order to be able to update Manekshaw.

Some 400 naval commandos and frogmen were trained. They were effective in attacking port facilities. Together with a Mukti Bahini gunboat mounting a Bofors 40 mm gun they captured, sank or damaged some 15 Pakistani ships, 11 coasters, 7 gunboats, 11 barges, 2 tankers and 19 river craft. These were, in fact, the most significant achievements of the Mukti Bahini.

Since the Mukti Bahini later would need more craft to convert into gunboats in the event of full scale hostilities, we approached the West Bengal Government for assistance. They were most helpful and gave us two craft on loan, MV *Palash* from the Calcutta Port Trust, and MV *Padma*. Our workshops reinforced the decks and mounted Bofors L/60 anti-aircraft guns on them. Crews for these were to be found from amongst Bengali Naval personnel of the Pakistani Navy. Cmdr Samant of the Indian Navy, an outstanding submariner, was assigned to assist. The Task Force was, in the event of war, to operate directly under the orders of Eastern Command at Fort William and not Eastern Naval Command. Later, when operations commenced, these two gunboats operated with considerable success. The Task Force was ordered to attack Pakistani shipping at the anchorages of Chalna Mangla. Samant wanted to attack Khulna but was told that he should not proceed beyond Chalna Mangla as our ground troops would be attacking Khulna and there were considerable Pakistani forces at Khulna. He was also apprised of the bomb line given to the Air Force. Khulna was included in that bomb line. Advance Headquarters Eastern Air Command asked me to inform Samant to paint the superstructures yellow as identification. As soon as this was done the squadrons operating there were informed. The Task Force consisting of the *Padma* and *Palash* and manned by the Mukti Bahini had considerable success. On the night of 9/10 December, it approached Mangla and entered the anchorage on 10 December. Samant in his overeagerness, decided to attack Khulna. Unfortunately, the Air Force failed to identify the vessels though they were clearly painted yellow. The craft were attacked and sunk in what is called, NATO terminology, 'friendly fire'. Samant and the crew were able to swim ashore. The Mukti Bahini were in control in that area and fortunately there were no casualties. Even so, we at Eastern Command recommended Samant for the award of the Mahavir Chakra for his action.

For guerrilla operations to flourish they must strike deep and firm roots in the population. For this time and organization are just as important as motivation. No guerrilla operations can produce quick results. Since it was apparent, however, that there was not unlimited time available and full-scale operations were likely to be undertaken in the future, it was necessary to access the number of guerrillas that needed to be trained during the six to seven months we had assessed as being at our disposal.

The untrained individuals enrolled by the Mukti Bahini were not familiar with arms and explosives. They should have been given a minimum of three months training in order to grasp the essentials of guerrilla warfare. A leader would take considerable longer to train. Yet guerrilla fighters were trained in large numbers within a period of three to four weeks, and as was to be expected, their effectiveness, due to no fault of theirs, was limited.

Specially selected, trained, dedicated and motivated leaders are essential for any successful guerrilla operations. Unfortunately, the selection was somewhat haphazard and sufficient time was not devoted to the training of leaders. The lack of junior leadership was keenly felt during the Mukti Bahini operations.

Three out of the five regular battalions were withdrawn from the preliminary operations in order to form them into a brigade. Later, three more battalions and two more brigade headquarters were raised. This, however, did not pay immediate dividends. In fact, potential leaders who could have been utilized for guerrilla operations were absorbed into the regular cadre. They carried out some well executed peripheral operations, in the areas around Sylhet and as part of a force that moved to capture Chittagong. The results achieved by the regular troops from East Bengal Regiments were substantial. Had this manpower and leadership been utilized to make up hard-core guerrilla forces they would have achieved much better results. Osmani gave greater priority to the raising of regular units rather than guerrilla forces.

Guerrilla operations require careful planning, briefing, induction and control. The Mukti Bahini sector headquarters were inadequately staffed to carry out these functions. The large numbers involved meant that detailed planning was not possible and induction was not properly organized. The monthly induction targets were unrealistic so that induction into the interior was generally haphazard. It was extremely difficult for the Headquarters of the Mukti Bahini to control such operations in the interior due to lack of adequate leadership and training and the deficiencies in signal equipment and communications. Some elements of the Mukti Bahini gravitated back towards the border areas.

It is essential that guerrilla forces are sufficiently motivated and determined to operate independently if so required. There was, sometimes, a tendency for guerrilla forces to wait for the Indian Army to carry out their tasks for them and not commit themselves fully in operations. An example of this attitude was Siddiqui's failure to intercept elements of withdrawing Pakistani forces from Mymensingh and Jamalpur. Another was the failure of the freedom fighters in Dacca to organize a World War II Maquis-type uprising.

The achievements of the Bangladesh forces and guerrillas were, nevertheless, a key factor in the liberation struggle. Despite the limitations of training and lack of junior leadership, they contributed substantially to the defeat of Pakistani forces in East Bengal. They achieved significant results in occupation of areas in the interior, demolitions and harassment. They completely demoralized the Pakistani Army, lowering their morale and creating such a hostile environment that their ability to operate was restricted and they were virtually confined to their fortified locations. The overall achievements of the Mukti Bahini and the East Bengal Regiments were enormous. Bangladeshis can be proud of them. Their contribution was a crucial element in the operations prior to and during full scale hostilities. Due credit must be given to their dedicated efforts to achieve the independence of their country.

American and Chinese Moves

Throughout the period prior to hostilities there was much talk of possible Chinese intervention. However, no Chinese build up was noticed in Tibet. Chinese strengths and dispositions, according to our assessment in Eastern Command, were not designed for any immediate offensive. Most of the Himalayan passes would, in any case, be impossible to cross in December and January. The Army Chief's assessment however, aided by Soviet advice, was that the Chinese were likely to intervene in the event of hostilities and Gen Manekshaw was unduly influenced by these Soviet views. The Americans, too, added to the confusion. Henry Kissinger, summoning the Indian Ambassador to the USA, L K Jha, warned that in the event of an Indo-Pakistan war and in the event of the Chinese supporting Pakistan, Washington would not come to the aid of India. In an urgent telegram to the Indian Government, Jha reported that while Kissinger 'did not know what the Chinese would do, it would be unsafe for us to assume that they would not come to Pakistan's help'.

We still had to find the troops for the Dacca thrust and time was running out. I discussed the matter with the Director of Military Operations, particularly the role we intended for 167 and 5 Mountain Brigades. The 123 Mountain Brigade had also been moved down in reserve. At the end of November I briefed the Army Commander regarding the moves of these brigades and their operational role. He told me to inform Army Headquarters officially. I replied that Inder Gill was in the picture but Gen Manekshaw had not been informed by Gill. Manekshaw, apprehensive that the Chinese would intervene once hostilities broke out, would never agree to withdrawal of troops from the Chinese border. He then replied that he himself would send a personal message to Manekshaw. I again requested him not to do so. He however sent a personal signal to Manekshaw. The reply came within two hours:

I have nursed you better than any woman. Who told you to move these brigades down? You will move them back at once.

Brig Sethna, the Brigadier General Staff and Lt Col Dal Singh came into my office with the message. I sent it to the Army Commander. The Army Commander walked into my office, somewhat shaken. I told him not to worry and that I would sort it out with the DMO, Inder Gill. I telephoned Inder and told him that we could not move the brigades back as it would take weeks to get them back for operations. On the other hand I was quite sure that eventually we would be able to convince Manekshaw that the Chinese would not intervene. Inder Gill agreed, but made me promise that we would not employ them in East Pakistan without his clearance. Later, on 8 December, after repeated requests, Manekshaw, realizing at last that the Chinese would not intervene, relented and agreed to let us employ 167 and 5 Mountain Brigades. Earlier on 6 December at Inder's request 123 Mountain Brigade was moved by air and rail to Western Command to reinforce that theatre as operations there were not going too well. Inder Gill once again displayed his capacity to assess situations, shoulder responsibility and act decisively.

International opinion was slowly beginning to turn in favour of the liberation movement. Foreign correspondents had

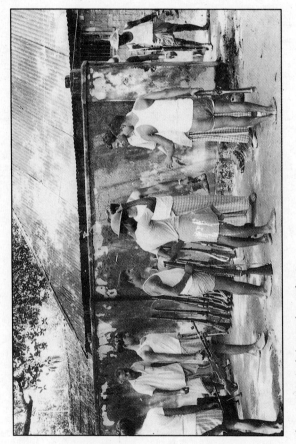

6. Members of the Mukti Bahini

7. Young Bangladeshi men under training

8. Mukti Bahini in action

9. Pakistani Chaffee tanks which were destroyed at Bayra

seen the refugee camps and been into Bangladesh. They deplored the atrocities and many of them viewed with favour the formation of an independent Bangladesh. Nearly all Islamic countries and China, however, supported the Pakistani position.

The stance of the United States, too, was pro-Pakistan. During the 1965 war with Pakistan China had made threatening moves on the Himalayan border and we still had to assess Chinese intentions this time. On 6 July Dr Henry Kissinger visited Delhi enroute to Islamabad. Yahya Khan used his good offices to arrange for Dr Kissinger to visit Beijing when Dr Kissinger made arrangements for President Nixon to visit China.

This Pakistani diplomatic initiative significantly increased American support to Pakistan, who pressed for action in the United Nations. U Thant prepared a plan for the stationing of United Nations observers. The Secretary General's proposals caused great concern as it would in effect have ensured the retention of West Pakistani control over East Pakistan. As Chinese and American support for Pakistan grew, the possibility of Chinese military intervention in the event of hostilities with Pakistan increased. On the initiative of Mrs Gandhi, who was pragmatic and resolute throughout this crisis, feelers were sent to Moscow through D P Dhar regarding a treaty of friendship, which the latter had been mooting since 1969 when he was Ambassador at Moscow. The Soviet response was quick and favourable. It was indeed a diplomatic breakthrough that a friendship treaty was drafted in a form that was almost tailor-made to meet Indian requirements, without comprising Indian sovereignty or its commitment to a non-aligned policy. The core element of the treaty is contained in Article IX which states, 'In the event of either being subjected to an attack or a threat thereof, the High Contracting Parties shall immediately enter into mutual consultations in order to remove any threat and to take appropriate effective measures to ensure peace and the security of their countries.' This was indeed a breakthrough giving India much more freedom of action in countering the hostile posture of China and to some extent the United States of America (see Appendix 17).

Meanwhile, the External Affairs Ministry in Delhi stepped up the degree of liaison with the Bangladesh Government in 'Mujibnagar' in Calcutta. A K Ray, a joint secretary in the Ministry, was sent to Calcutta for this purpose. Ray was a capable officer who was well-acquainted with the current situation. He was practical in his approach and established a good rapport with the Bangladeshi leadership.

D P Dhar was the head of the policy planning division in the Ministry of External Affairs. The External Affairs Ministry was largely ignored and foreign policy was formulated by a very competent and influential group of Kashmiris, pro-Soviet in their views: D P Dhar, Foreign Secretary T N Kaul, P N Haksar, and P N Dhar. This powerful group was unkindly often referred to as the 'Kashmiri Mafia'. D P was sympathetic to the pro-Soviet elements in Mujibnagar. From the end of August, whenever D P Dhar visited Calcutta he operated out of the owner's suite in the Grand Hotel. I had known D P Dhar earlier in Kashmir and he invited me for discussions several times to his suite. Our meetings were spread out over several hours and interspersed periodically by shorter meetings with many others. His views on Communists were revealing. According to him pro-Soviet Communists were 'good guys' and the Marxists, in East Pakistan were not. I tried to argue that these groups should not be supported either politically or militarily. His answer was always 'Jake, I know what I am doing'. He bypassed A K Ray, which was indeed unfortunate. I last met with Dhar a few days after the surrender, at the VIP lounge of Calcutta airport. I suggested to Dhar that it was important to get from the Bangladesh Government an agreement on what I considered to be the three essentials: guarantees for the Hindu minority, rationalization of the enclaves, and transit rights by rail and inland waterways through Bangladesh with use of facilities at Chittagong port. D P, with his charmingly disarming smile, turned around and said, 'Jake, you are a soldier. These problems are political. They can be sorted out at the appropriate time.' I replied that the appropriate time was now and it would be very difficult later to obtain any agreements. He smiled again. The Chief Minister of West Bengal was present at this meeting but did not respond.

The Mukti Bahini operations were stepped up from September and became better organized and more effective. They began to have a demoralizing effect on the Pakistani Government in Dacca and also the Pakistani Army, particularly the enlisted men, who were becoming increasingly disenchanted with their cause and their officers.

Pakistani efforts at the United Nations and with the Chinese were not gaining for them the support they expected. Their efforts to get a firm commitment of action from China in case India attacked, failed. The Chinese stance was ambivalent, perhaps because the Chinese, pragmatic as ever, had accepted the reality of the coming independence of Bangladesh and did not wish to jeopardize a future relationship. The American position was more complex. Dr Kissinger asserted that he had privately indicated to India that he felt that the political autonomy of East Bengal was inevitable though Ambassador Keating in Delhi apparently was not aware of any such advice according to his statement in the *New York Herald Tribune*, 6 January 1972. I later asked L K Jha, who was then our Ambassador in Washington about this and he, too, said that he was unaware of it (see Appendix 19).

Ambassador Keating visited Fort William during this period. The Army Commander being out on tour, I apprised him of the current situation, particularly the refugee problem and the large-scale atrocities being perpetrated by the Pakistanis. I told him that I was at a loss to understand why the Government of the world's most powerful democracy should support a brutal, repressive, military regime which had completely disregarded the results of the elections in East Pakistan. Keating was a polished diplomat. His sensitive face coloured slightly but he did not resent what I said and did not defend his Government's stance either. Perhaps his relations with the State Department and Dr Kissinger were not sufficiently close to counter Nixon's tilt towards Pakistan.

War

At approximately 1740 hours on 3 December our airfields in the west were bombed by the Pakistani Air Force. The bombing effort was spread over several airfields but the damage caused was minimal. To this day I cannot understand the logic behind its timing or method. Richard Sisson and Leo Rose, in their book *War and Secession*, suggest that Yahya Khan's decision to declare war was based on three considerations. First, there was the military commander's sensitivity to the adverse publicity Pakistan was receiving in the Western press, which portrayed them as 'nitwits' or idiots rendered powerless by India. Second, Indian action in East Pakistan had not evoked suitable international response in favour of Pakistan. Third, there were Bhutto's taunts to Yahya that if he did nothing he would be 'lynched by the people'. On 30 November the decision to wage war on India was taken. D-Day was fixed for 2 December but was later postponed by a day.

At 1800 hours on 3 December I was in the office when I received a telephone call from Gen Manekshaw. He told me that Pakistani aircrafts were bombing our airfields in the west and that I was to inform the Prime Minister, Mrs Indira Gandhi, who was then staying at Raj Bhawan in Calcutta. I asked him if we could put our contingency plans into operation and he told me to go ahead. As far as he was concerned all-out war had started. This, he said, should also be conveyed to the Prime Minister, adding that he would be

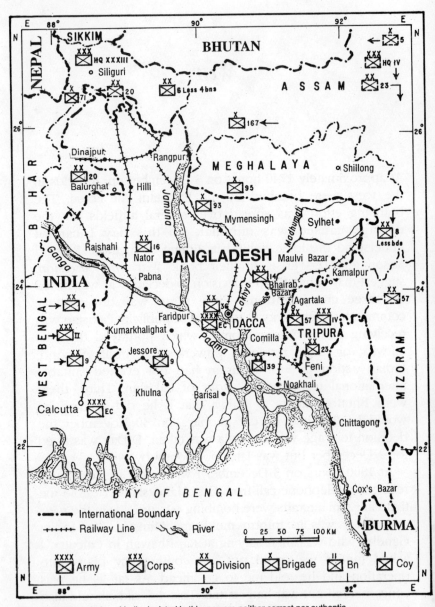

The external boundaries of India depicted in this map are neither correct nor authentic.

MAP 1: INITIAL DEPLOYMENT AND MOVES TO CONCENTRATION AREAS

issuing confirmatory orders immediately. I walked into Lt Gen Aurora's office through the connecting swing door between our offices and informed him of the conversation. Even though Manekshaw had detailed me to brief the Prime Minister, I suggested that it would be more appropriate for him to do so while I got the necessary orders issued and tied up the air support. He agreed and went to meet the Prime Minister.

Fortunately, getting the Staff together was not a problem as everyone was working late. The Advance Air Headquarters were informed that I would be coming to the JAAOC to coordinate the air support and the Staff issued the necessary orders. I briefed all corps commanders telephonically. The allocation of the air effort was made at the JAAOC and sorties allotted to corps. Pakistani airfield runways were a priority target. At around 2030 hours, orders and coordination for commencement of the offensive were completed. Aurora had just returned from briefing the Prime Minister and as I briefed him on the action taken, there was a feeling of relief all around. The troops were impatient and eager to unleash the offensive. As far as we, at Command Headquarters, were concerned, the infrastructure was ready, the logistical build up was as near as possible complete and operation plans had been made in detail, discussed and 'war gamed'. Aurora was exceedingly cheerful and asked his ADC to get a bottle of whisky from the mess. We realized that for some days to come there would be very little rest for anyone.

As we made the most of our few moments of leisure, I had a call from Sydney Schanberg, correspondent of the *New York Times*. Schanberg asked me what we were doing in the light of the Pakistani attacks in the west. I lightheartedly told him that we were having a drink. He asked whether we were anxious. I told him that we, in the Eastern Army, were confident that we would liberate Bangladesh in a short time. He wanted me to ensure that he would be allowed to accompany our leading troops to Dacca. I promised him I would do what I could. Later, in the final stages of the war, Schanberg walked into Dacca with the patrols of IV Corps.

Earlier on the morning of 3 December Adm Krishnan, Flag Officer Commanding in Chief of our Eastern Naval Command telephoned me to say that the wreckage of a Pakistani submarine had been found by fishermen on the approaches to the Vishakhapatnam Port. We had signal intercepts of the *Ghazi*, a Pakistani submarine, entering the Bay of Bengal. We had passed on this information to the Indian Navy. Krishnan said that the blowing up of the *Ghazi* either on 1 or 2 December whilst laying mines was an act of God. He said it would permit the Navy greater freedom of action. Next morning, on 4 December, Krishnan again telephoned asking me whether we had reported the blowing up of the *Ghazi* to Delhi. I said that we had not as I presumed that he had done so. Relieved, he thanked me and asked me to forget our previous conversation. The official Naval version given out later was that the *Ghazi* had been sunk by the ships of the Eastern Fleet on 4 December.

Progress of Operations

Fall of Jessore

By the time full-scale hostilities commenced on 4 December 1971, 9 Infantry Division found itself fully engaged against Pakistani defences. The defences of Jessore had by now been strengthened by linking up various marshes in the area and by pulling in troops which had earlier occupied the Chaugacha area and by flying in a battalion from the Rajshahi area. The operations of 9 Infantry Division were, therefore, reduced to series of hammering attacks in order to achieve a breakthrough. We had suggested, as early as 28 November, that the Division could modify its defensive posture around Bayra by moving forward and attempting to use the Chaugacha–Hakimpur–Jessore and Mithapukhuria–Lebutala–Jessore axis but apparently this they were slow in doing as they were apprehensive of a counter attack. In view of this stalemate, on 5 December I spoke to Maj Gen Inder Gill, Director Military Operations, requesting him to let us use the Amy Headquarters reserve of 50 Parachute Brigade, less one battalion group, which was to drop at Tangail. Inder, helpful as ever, agreed straightway but with the proviso that when required by him they were to revert to Army Headquarters control. I agreed and immediately sent for Brig Mathew Thomas, Commander 50 Parachute Brigade and briefed him on his mission to capture Jessore from the rear and also

105

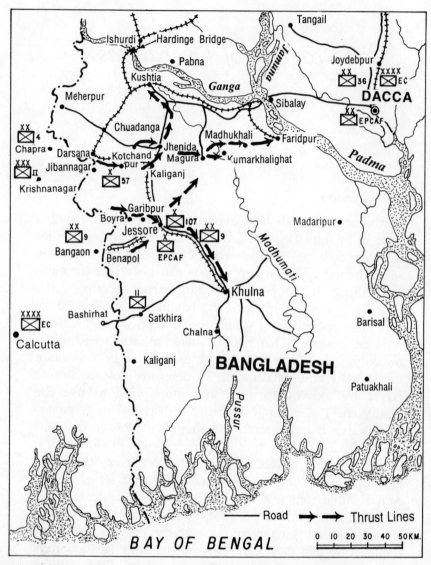

The external boundaries of India depicted in this map are neither correct nor authentic.

MAP 2: WESTERN SECTOR

indicated the thrust line. We also arranged to let him have another battalion. I informed Lt Gen Raina of II Corps of this and requested him to give Thomas all assistance. The Brigade, less a battalion, moved on 6 December to carry out its tasks. The 9 Infantry Division was, however, spurred on to push into Jessore before 50 Parachute Brigade could get there. The Pakistanis, having earlier decided to vacate Jessore and pulled back to prepared positions at Daulatpur, Khulna and east of the Madhumati river, the Brigade group was not used for the breakthrough on 6 December in area Durga Barkati, on Chaugacha–Jessore road. Jessore was occupied by the afternoon of 7 December. Niazi's signal intercept organization had picked up transmissions for the move of 50 Para Brigade but were unable to interpret them correctly. A CBS radio report that 5000 paratroops had been seen at Dum Dum airport convinced Niazi after the air drop of a battalion group that the whole of 50 Parachute Brigade had dropped at Tangail. In the meanwhile, 9 Infantry Division was to have sent a force from Jessore to Magura to reinforce 4 Mountain Division's thrust to Faridpur. The 9 Infantry Division decided instead, contrary to the plan, to regroup and after a pause to divert its thrust to Khulna. We therefore ordered 50 Para Brigade to move on the Magura axis. A battalion of the Brigade suffered heavy casualties in the process. The 4 Mountain Division were also spurred onto take Magura.

Stalemate at Khulna

After the capture of Jessore, 32 Infantry Brigade of 9 Infantry Division commenced the advance to Khulna. The enemy had prepared a series of delaying position in the built-up area of Ramnagar, Singla, Nawapara and Phultala. The terrain astride the road on this axis was marshy. The enemy engaged in stiff delaying actions and demolished a large number of bridges and culverts during withdrawal. However, the delaying positions were pushed back one by one. Some outflanking moves were possible but progress was slow. The main enemy defences at Daulatpur were contacted on 11 December. Daulatpur is an extension of Khulna and the two together formed a continuous narrow and long built up belt of about two miles. It could not be readily bypassed because it was flanked on the west by marshes and on the east by the Bhairab river. The Pakistanis had apparently intended to fight to the last in this last ditch fortress and the operation for the capture of Daulatpur and Khulna, therefore, turned into a hard slogging match. The Pakistanis fought over every bit of ground. Despite our plan of operations, and contrary to our instructions, the whole of 9 Infantry Division unnecessarily became committed to this area instead of concentrating on its specified thrust line to Magura–Faridpur. A series of attacks were launched in which both sides suffered heavy casualties. Up to the morning of 16 December the Division had managed to capture only three of the forward enemy localities at Siramani East, Siramani West and Syamganj. On the morning of 16 December, when I was changing helicopters at Jessore en route to Dacca, to arrange for the surrender, I saw an air observation aircraft sortie about to take off. The artillery pilot informed me that he was going to engage targets in the Khulna area. I immediately got on to the radio set and instructed the Division to stop this unnecessary fighting as they well knew that the cease fire had already come into force the previous afternoon, and that I was on my way to arrange for the surrender of all forces. Earlier, 42 Infantry Brigade attempted an outflanking move by crossing the Bhairab river to the west, and establishing themselves on the main road. The first crossing was made with the help of boats marshalled with the help of the Mukti Bahini on the night of 13/14 December. The Brigade moved south up to the river junction without much opposition.

During the second crossing, however, they met with stiff opposition. The crossing was still in progress when orders for suspension of operations were given.

The 4 Mountain Division captured Darsana and Kotchandpur by 5 December. Instead of capturing Kaliganj and then advancing to Jhenida along the main road axis, the Division executed a brilliant cross-country thrust towards the north. A battalion squadron road block was established between Chaugacha and Jhenida. Several attempts made by the enemy to break through this block were foiled. The forces west of the block, instead of reinforcing Jhenida, had to withdraw north towards Kushtia. The 41 Mountain Brigade approached Jhenida along a very difficult track—Kotchandpur–Talsar–Jhenida. Jhenida fell comparatively easily on the afternoon of 7 December. Magura fell on 8 December and the Madhumati ferry was contacted. The para drop of two companies planned for this area was, thus, not required.

Crossing of Madhumati

After the capture of Magura, 62 Mountain Brigade commenced the advance towards Faridpur. The Pakistanis had demolished the bridge over Kumar river and had withdrawn east of the Madhumati, leaving a delaying force in the Majail area west of the river. The Brigade, after clearing this opposition, concentrated on the west bank of the Madhumati. By the last light of 9 December it had commenced preparations for the crossing. In the meantime 7 Mountain Brigade column, which had been sent to Kushtia, ran into trouble with a depleted enemy brigade and a squadron of Pakistani light tanks which had been positioned there with the intention of launching a disruptive attack from the north. The enemy in this strength was not expected at Kushtia and 7 Mountain Brigade was, therefore, taken somewhat unawares. We lost five tanks and the vanguard

109

company suffered heavy casualties. The 4 Mountain Division thereupon overreacted, and instead of pressing on with the advance on the thrust line across the Madhumati on 9 December diverted to Kushtia. When the Hardinge Bridge was contacted on 12 December, it was found that the Pakistanis had withdrawn and partially demolished the bridge. This setback would not have occurred had II Corps agreed to our suggested thrust line of Shikarpur–Kushtia. The Hardinge Bridge could have been taken intact and the withdrawal of Pakistani troops across the river would not have taken place. More serious was the delay caused in getting the Division back onto its original thrust line. When I asked Raina to concentrate on his main thrust, he replied that he was unaware of the quantum of troops diverted by 4 Mountain Division from their primary task. Consequently, the advance to Faridpur was delayed by at least three days and the contingency plan of crossing the Padma at Goalundo Ghat to Dacca could not be put into effect. The II Corps also failed to ensure that 9 Infantry Division send a force on the Jessore–Magura axis as originally ordered and acquiesced to the Division dissipating its potential by trying to expedite the capture of the low priority objective of Khulna. The IWT Flotilla reported to II Corps a short distance upstream of the Hardinge Bridge on 5 December. There they remained anchored until they were moved to Dacca on 18 December. When I tried to persuade Raina to utilize them by moving them down to Faridpur he stated that he could not do so due to small arms fire from the north bank. I told him that for several years I had gone to school crossing the bridge and know that it was not possible to see the opposite bank due to the width of the river. He did not respond. It was clear that he was not keen to proceed beyond the Padma–Brahamaputra. Thus the possibility of taking Dacca from this sector could not be availed of (see Appendix 4).

The area of Kushtia and Bheramara having been cleared,

attention was again switched to the crossing of the Madhumati. By 13 December 62 Mountain Brigade was concentrated west of the river and by the next day 7 Mountain Brigade was concentrated at Magura. The river was a major obstacle, approximately 500 yards wide and at places more than 40 feet deep. A deep salient towards the east results in the road west of the ferry site being flanked by the river to a distance of about two miles in the north and four miles in the south. The enemy was holding the eastern bank with approximately two weak battalions supported by one battery of 105 mm guns organized into an ad hoc brigade under the Colonel General Staff of their 9 Infantry Division. The original plan was for 62 Mountain Brigade to cross the river in the north, outflank the main enemy position and capture Kumarkhali, on the main road. After further consideration it was decided that both 62 and 7 Mountain Brigades should be employed, one each on the northern and the southern flanks, and with a pincer movement cut the road east of the ferry. Both Brigades crossed the river in country boats on the night of 14/15 December against stiff opposition. The task of 7 Mountain Brigade was particularly difficult as they had not had enough time for reconnaissance and had to make an approach march of about 30 kilometres cross-country to reach the river line. The crossing was, however, very successful and the pincers closed in on the main road by the afternoon of 15 December. After a few desperate, unsuccessful attempts at breaking out, the enemy force surrendered with all personnel and weapons. The delay caused on this axis by the failure of II Corps to control 4 Mountain Division and to acquiesce to 9 Infantry Division's diverting troops from the thrust line Jessore–Magura to Khulna, together with the non-utilization of their Inland Waterways Flotilla cost us the chance to take Dacca from this thrust line.

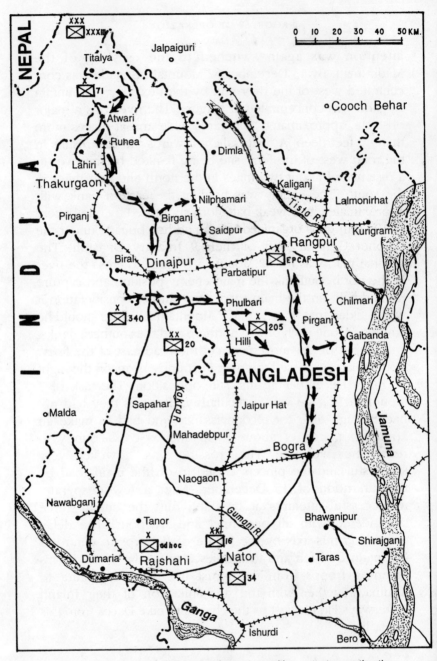

The external boundaries of India depicted in this map are neither correct nor authentic.

MAP 3: NORTH-WESTERN SECTOR

NORTH-WESTERN SECTOR

The 71 Mountain Brigade, which had by itself advanced all the way down from Mirgarh and captured Pachagarh and Thakurgaon before 3 December, continuted to advance south, captured Birganj on 5 December and contacted the Kantanagar Bridge over the Dhepa river on 6 December. The enemy had, as expected, blown the bridge and was holding the area between Dhepa and Atrai rivers in strength. The Brigade tried to cross the river but suffered heavy casualties. On the night of 9/10 December, a battalion block was established south of the enemy position towards Dinajpur but this did not impede the enemy as his lines of maintenance were from the east. After this, the Brigade continued to threaten Dinajpur from the north by sending out patrols right up to its outskirts till it was ordered to change its major thrust line to the east, towards Nilphamari. It crossed the Dhepa river about ten miles further north and captured Khansama on 13 December. Another enemy opposition in the area was cleared four miles further east on 14 December. By the morning of 16 December the Brigade had reached about 5 miles south-west of Nilphamari. As a result of the relentless pressure by 71 Mountain Brigade, the Pakistanis did not, until the last, risk thinning out their strongholds at Saidpur, Rangpur, Paravatipur and Dinajpur to reinforce the threatened areas further south.

The Threat to Rangpur

The 9 Mountain Brigade of 6 Mountain Division captured Kurigram and Lalmanirhat by 6 December and continued to pose a threat to Rangpur from these directions. Later, the Brigade was moved to the area south of Dinajpur to relieve 340 Mountain Brigade of 20 Mountain Division for offensive operations.

Securing of the Hilli-Gaibanda 'Waistline'

The 20 Mountain Division had positioned 165 Mountain Brigade to hold a firm base in the Balurghat Bulge: 340 Mountain Brigade for investing Dinajpur from the south, and 66 and 202 Mountain Brigades for the main thrust to Pirganj. The 66 Mountain Brigade captured Phulbari, but 202 Mountain Brigade, which was ordered to advance on the Hilli-Charkhai axis could not proceed beyond Hilli. The 66 Mountain Brigade was, therefore, ordered to capture Charkhai also, which they did on 4 December. The 66 Mountain Brigade commenced advance on the track to Pirganj and captured Nawabganj and Hathangi ferry by 5 December and Kanchandha ferry by 6 December. The 340 Mountain Brigade was relieved by 9 Mountain Brigade, so that the momentum of advance to Pirganj could be built up.

On 7 December, 66 Mountain Brigade was ordered to contact Ghoraghat from the west, while 340 Mountain Brigade captured Pirganj and contacted Ghoraghat from north-east. The 66 Mountain Brigade met with stiff opposition at Bhaduria, held by two infantry companies and one troop of armour. It took them up to 11 December to clear this opposition with 82 enemy dead when counted. The 17 Kumaon, which had attacked, suffered 55 killed and 72 wounded.

The 340 Mountain Brigade made a rapid advance, captured Pirganj on 7 December, Palashbari on 9 December and Gaibanda and Phulchari ferry on 10 December, securing the 'waistline' and isolating Pakistani forces in the Dinajpur–Rangpur belt. The Brigade pressed on further south and captured Gobindganj on 11 December with a brilliant enveloping move. A complete battalion with three tanks and five 105 mm guns was captured or annihilated. In the meantime, the Pakistanis continued to fight resolutely from their strong defences between Hilli and Ghoraghat. Hilli

114

finally fell on 11 December and Ghoraghat on 12 December. The Pakistanis also launched fierce counterattacks on Pirganj from the north in an effort to open the road but met with no success.

Advance to Bogra

After the 'waistline' was secured, plans were made for securing Bogra by advancing on two axis: 340 Mountain Brigade on Gobindganj–Bogra axis and 202 Mountain Brigade on Ghoraghat–Khetlal–Bogra axis. The 165 Mountain Brigade was to simultaneously make a limited advance to Jaipurhat. The 165 Mountain Brigade captured Panchbibi against spirited fight-back from the Pakistanis on 13 December but Jaipurhat was occupied unopposed. A column of 202 Mountain Brigade advancing on the Ghoraghat–Saidpur–Khetlal axis captured Khetlal on 12 December after overcoming stiff opposition. The advance beyond Khetlal was not found to be possible as the track had been extensively demolished. The 340 Mountain Brigade, however, made a rapid advance. The bridge over the Ichamati river held by one enemy company was captured intact by yet another well executed enveloping move on 13 December. The bridge on the Karatoya river was also captured intact and Bogra contacted. The Pakistanis resisted to the last in the built-up area of Bogra, which was held by remnants of the 205 Infantry Brigade. By the time operations were suspended. The 340 Mountain Brigade had captured 20 officers and 500 other ranks and secured the northern parts of Bogra.

Advance to Rangpur

On 14 December 66 Mountain Brigade, followed by 202 Mountain Brigade were ordered to advance to Rangpur. Mitapukur was captured against light opposition on

115

15 December and by the time the orders for suspension of action were given, Rangpur had been invested from the south-west and south by the two Brigades.

Even though 20 Mountain Division had the heaviest opposition to clear, it had executed its operations most creditably.

SOUTH-EASTERN SECTOR

Isolation of Sylhet

The 59 Mountain Brigade of 8 Mountain Division had been held up at Kalaura since 1 December. Kalaura fell on 6 December after air power was used to flush out the enemy. By 5 December 81 Mountain Brigade had captured Munshi Bazar and on 7 December, after heavy resistance, they isolated the Maulvi Bazar defences. The Pakistani 313 Infantry Brigade was ordered to move from Maulvi Bazar to Sylhet. On 10 December 81 Mountain Brigade captured Saidpur and Sherpur ferries, unopposed, thus blocking the only road link south-west of Sylhet. Thereafter they concentrated at Agartala as corps reserve.

On 7 December, 4/5 GR of 59 Mountain Brigade had been lifted by helicopters to south-east of Sylhet across the Surma river. The Pakistanis had evacuated the civilian population from Sylhet and fortified the town. The defences were held by Pakistani 202 Infantry Brigade. Pakistani 311 Infantry Brigade, ex-Maulvi Bazar, joined the Sylhet garrison, bringing the strength up to six battalions, one regiment of 105 mm guns and one battery of 120 mm.

The move of the Pakistani 311 Infantry Brigade from Maulvi Bazar to Sylhet had not been anticipated by us at Command Headquarters and came as a surprise. We had expected this Brigade would fall back to the Coronation Bridge on the Meghna for the defence of the Meghna crossing and Dacca. Had they done so IV Corps' progress

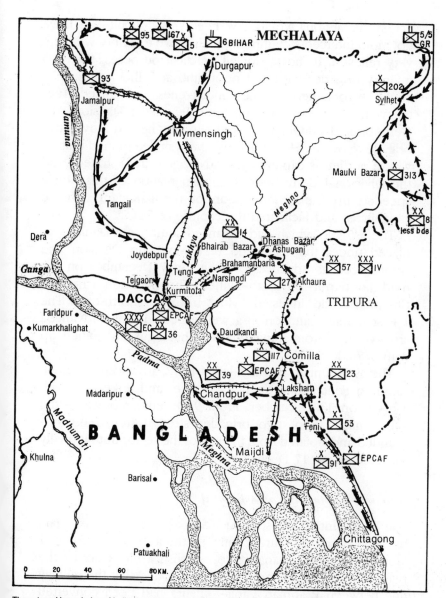

The external boundaries of India depicted in this map are neither correct nor authentic.

MAP 4: NORTHERN AND SOUTH-EASTERN SECTORS

across the Meghna would have been very difficult. When we got radio intercepts confirming their move to Sylhet we were very relieved. It meant, for all practical purposes, that two infantry brigades were out on a limb at Sylhet where they could be contained and their effectiveness neutralized. After the war, whilst interrogating the GOC of the Division, Maj Gen Abdul Majid Quazi, I asked him why he had moved this brigade to Sylhet. He replied that he was determined that he would not let us capture Sylhet. Niazi's fortress strategy and the Divisional Commander's implementation of this policy speeded up the disintegration of the Pakistani defence capabilities and facilitated the capture of Dacca.

The 5/5 GR, which had advanced south from Dauki, was placed under the command of 8 Mountain Division and commenced its advance to Sylhet on 7 December on the road Jaintiapur–Darbasth–Sylhet. The battalion captured Chandghat and invested Sylhet from the north-east. The 1 East Bengal Battalion in a well executed move advanced cross-country from Kanairghat to Chiknagul and joined up with 5/5 GR.

The 59 Mountain Brigade, less 4/5 GR, advanced to Sylhet, captured Fenchuganj on 11 December and linked up with 4/5 GR on 13 December. From 9 December onwards the Sylhet garrison of two brigades strength remained surrounded and isolated from the rest of the sector until it finally surrendered on 17 December.

Advance to Meghna at Ashuganj

The 57 Mountain Division encircled and captured Ashuganj by 5 December. During this battle a battalion of 311 Mountain Brigade managed to establish a block across the river Titas, in general area Koda, and found that the railway line between Brahman Baria–Akhaura had been converted into a road by removing the rails. Not only was the railway bridge over the Titas intact, a further probe towards Brahman Baria indicated that it was lightly held. We had initially not considered advancing on this axis to Dacca as we had expected Brahman Baria to be strongly held and elements of the brigade from Maulvi Bazar were also expected to withdraw to this area. Moreover, there was no known road communication between Brahman Baria and Ashuganj. However, since the Pakistani 311 Infantry Brigade had moved north to Sylhet, a road axis now existed. On the recommendation of the GOC, Ben Gonsalves, supported by his Corps Commander, it was agreed to change the thrust line of 57 Mountain Division to Brahman Baria–Ashuganj instead of towards Daudkandi.

The Division, less one brigade, made a three-pronged approach over the water-logged terrain. However, by the time the pincers closed the enemy had slipped out of Brahman Baria. The Division contacted Ashuganj on 9 December but by then the enemy had, as expected, blown up the Coronation Bridge and pulled back to Bhairab Bazar leaving only small pockets of resistance at Ashuganj.

Advance to the Meghna

The 61 Mountain Brigade, directly under Headquarters Main IV Corps, had been given the task of crossing the Gumti river, cutting off the roads from the west and north-west and closing in on Maynamati from the west, to help 23 Mountain Division. On 7 December information was received that the enemy had withdrawn from the Burichang area. The 61 Mountain Brigade seized the opportunity boldly. The Brigade crossed the Gumti without any opposition and established blocks at Chandina and Jaffarganj. The Corps Engineers converted a subsidiary track from Srimantapur to Burichang up to the Gumti into a Class 5 track in 12 hours. The same track was converted into a Class 9 axis, including launching of a bridge over the river within 72 hours. The Brigade was thereafter maintained on this track throughout.

Meanwhile, 12 Kumaon with a troop of armour was pushed forward with speed to secure Daudkandi. No organized opposition was encountered en route, only minor opposition of a platoon strength at Elliotganj. The position was cleared and Daudkandi was secured on 9 December.

The Pakistanis were in confusion. Comilla town was vacated and occupied on 9 December. Whoever could, got into the fortress at Maynamati. About 1500 personnel, trying to withdraw to Maynamati were trapped between Comilla and Daudkandi and surrendered. This was the first major local surrender by Pakistani troops.

Envelopment of Laksham and Advance to Meghna at Chandpur

The reinforced Pakistani 117 Infantry Brigade was holding the area of Lalmai Hills south-west of Comilla–Laksham–Chaudagram-Mudafarganj in strength, leaving very little in depth. It was therefore decided to isolate Laksham, bypass the Lalmai defences and dash for Chandpur.

The 61 Mountain Brigade secured the northern flank by blocking the road in area Saugram. The 301 Mountain Brigade infiltrated between Lalmai Hills and Laksham on the night of 3 December and secured Mudafarganj by 6 December, capturing a complete battalion en route. The Pakistanis launched fierce counter attacks at Mudafarganj on the night of 7/8 December but could not dislodge us. The Brigade continued its advance, captured Hajiganj after stiff opposition on 8 December and reached Chandpur on the night of 9 December.

The 181 Mountain Brigade followed 301 Mountain Brigade and established itself on the routes north and west of Laksham. On 7 December the Pakistanis vacated the southern portion of Lalmai Hills, which was then occupied by 181 Mountain Brigade.

In the meantime, on the night of 3/4 December 83 Mountain Brigade had also infiltrated into the area and established blocks between Chaudagram and Laksham. Chaudagram was cleared on 5 December. The Laksham garrison withdrew to Maynamati and Laksham was occupied on 9 December.

Meghna Bulge Secured

By 9 December, our troops had reached all the three key points on the Meghna, i.e. Ashuganj, Daudkandi and Chandpur and secured the vital Meghna Bulge. The approaches to Dacca from the east lay open.

Investment of Maynamati

Maynamati had been prepared by the enemy as a strong fortress having three lines of defence with an anti-tank ditch skirting them. With the withdrawal of troops from Comilla, Laksham and Chaudagram areas approximately 4000 troops were concentrated in the cantonment, along with four tanks and a battery of artillery. Any attempt to reduce it by direct attack would have been very costly and I advised against it but the Corps Commander was determined to capture Maynamati cantonment.

By 9 December, however, this position had been bypassed and invested from both directions. The 61 Mountain Brigade closed in from the north and west, and was placed under the command of 23 Mountain Division. The 181 Mountain Brigade of 23 Mountain Division closed in from the south. The Maynamati garrison remained surrounded till 16 December when 86 officers, 175 junior commissioned officers and 4000 other ranks surrendered. Since Army

121

Headquarters had stipulated Chittagong as primary objective, though in our assessment its importance was peripheral, we had to find some troops to capture this subsidiary objective.

Code named 'Kilo', this force was created with two regular modified '1' Battalions from the Mizo Hills, two East Bengal Battalions, one BSF Battalion, one CRP Battalion, a Mountain Regiment, Mujib Battery and a BSF Post Group. This Force was eventually placed under Brig Anand Saroop of the Counter Insurgency School. We had planned for Brig Shabeg Singh with his Sector Headquarters to command this force. However, when instructed by Aurora to do so he flatly declined saying that it would have an adverse effect on his military reputation! Aurora acquiesced in his refusal. Due to our operations in Laksham area, Feni was vacated by the enemy and secured by Kilo Force on 6 December. The force also occupied Karrehat and Zorarganj by 8 December and then commenced its advance to Chittagong. The enemy at Sitakund was surrounded and the position cleared by 12 December. On the initiative of the Corps Commander, who was keen to speed up the capture of Chittagong, this force was reinforced with 83 Mountain Brigade which concentrated in the Sitakund area on 12 December. Kumarighat which was held by two enemy companies was cleared on the night of 13/14 December. The force had reached Faujdahat on the outskirts of Chittagong when operations were suspended.

On the morning of 14 December two Air Force Canberra pilots came to see me seeking a detailed briefing for a bombing attack on a strategic target in Tungi that had been selected by the Chiefs of Staff in Delhi. By then our troops had reached the outskirts of Tungi, which was within range of our fighter bomber aircraft. This target, a factory still under construction, had been put on the list of strategic targets some months earlier but had no military relevance at this stage. In the eastern part of the Theatre of operations our troops were approaching Chittagong, which was not within range of our fighter bomber aircraft. Aircraft from the carrier *Vikrant* were not in a position to support this thrust. In view of the overall situation I immediately diverted the strike to the enemy defences at Faujdahat on the approaches to Chittagong. The strike was successful. Late that night I received a telephone call from a very agitated Devasher, Senior Air Staff Officer at Headquarters Eastern Air Command, telling me that the Chief of the Air Staff in Delhi demanded to know who had the audacity to divert a strategic air strike that had been ordered by the three Chiefs of Staff in Delhi. I explained to Devasher the nature of the fluid and fast moving operations and that there was no time at all to observe the niceties of lengthy conventional procedures to get the Chiefs of Staff in Delhi to agree to a switch of targets. I told him that the pilots were not to blame and that I accepted full responsibility for this diversion. The Chief of the Air Staff, a practical and pragmatic officer, accepted the necessity for this diversion and I heard no more in this matter.

The Special Frontier Force under Maj Gen Sujan Singh Uban had also been made available. Manekshaw had been pressing us to integrate them into our offensive. I looked for an independent task for them. Since we had pulled out the two infantry battalions from Mizoram, I suggested that Sujan Singh's force should move from Mizoram into the Chittagong Hill tracts, capture Rangamati, which was held by some commandos and a few irregulars and pose a threat to Chittagong. The terrain was hilly and thickly forested and Sujan Singh's forces could quite easily carry out the tasks allotted to them. After the cease fire they moved to Chittagong from where they were transported back to India.

Abortive Amphibious Operation for Cox's Bazar

Gen Manekshaw telephoned me on 9 December ordering us to send a force by sea to Cox's Bazar to prevent Pakistani troops escaping from there into Burma. I told Gen Manekshaw that there was no indication of this, but he was adamant. I pointed out that we had no troops trained in amphibious operations, that there were no life belts, scrambling nets, or suitable landing craft and most importantly, the troops that he wanted us to send had never been to sea. He cut me short saying that he was not interested in excuses and these were the orders of the three Chiefs of Staff. I requested the Navy at Calcutta to locate a suitable merchant ship. Fortunately, the *Vishwa Vijay* had just discharged its cargo and I gave orders to requisition it. At the meeting in Eastern Command with the Navy we discussed the operation. I had taken part in several amphibious operations and was aware of the special equipment and training required. I had served in Burma during World War II and had trained for amphibious operations on the beaches stretching south of Cox's Bazar, I was familiar with the coast line and beaches there. The beach at Ukhia was gently sloping and there were a number of runnels on the approaches to the beaches. I brought this to the notice of the Navy. As life belts and other necessary equipment was not available and the troops to be used had not seen the sea, I persuaded the Navy to beach the landing craft and refloat them at high tide. The troops would then land dry shod. The Navy agreed, but later changed its plan with disastrous consequences at sea. The force was to be transported in a merchant ship that was to sail on 10 December and be in position by 12 December. Two LSTs were to transfer the troops from the merchant ship at sea and land them dry shod. The aircraft carrier *Vikrant* was to provide air and fire support. This force, code named 'Romeo', was hurriedly assembled. We earmarked

124

Headquarters of 8 Mountain Artillery Brigade commanded by Brig S S Rai, which was allotted to the II Corps, 1/3 GR, two companies of 11 Bihar and a detachment of artillery. A naval contingent of 150, which was to participate did not arrive. The force sailed from Calcutta on 12 December, two days behind schedule.

On 14 December, the Force, while still at sea, was transferred to INS *Gildar* and *Gharial*. As all planning had been done off the map, the actual survey of the beach was to be carried out on arrival. By now the Navy had also decided to change the agreed plan and attempted to disembark the troops by boat. No proper beach reconnaissance was carried out. I had also warned the Navy to watch out for runnels. Even so, one of the craft attempted to beach and ran straight into a runnel. Only 12 men could disembark and 2 of them drowned. With another effort, 30 men were put ashore. The aircraft carrier *Vikrant* did not participate. By then it was apparent that there were no enemy in the area, only a Mukti Bahini camp nearby. The force was eventually taken off the ships between 16 and 18 December with the help of local boats. We were lucky to get out of this ill-conceived hastily mounted operation without further losses. Other than a telephone call from the Army Chief, no written instructions had been issued by any of the Service Headquarters in Delhi. Amphibious operations require specialized equipment and craft, detailed planning, intensive training and rehersals by the participating personnel of the Army, Navy and Air Force. None of these prerequisites existed. They should not be mounted and launched in the cavalier manner ordered by the Chiefs of Staff at Delhi.

Northern Thrust and Para Drop

The enemy garrison at Kamalpur finally surrendered to 95 Mountain Brigade on 4 December. The advance was resumed and Jamalpur, although encircled by 7 December, held out until 11 December. Earlier, Brig Kler had sent a message to Lt Col Sultan to surrender. Sultan sent back a defiant reply, enclosing a bullet in his letter. The letter, surely, deserves a place in military history and has, therefore, been reproduced in Appendix 3.

The 167 and 5 Mountain Brigades were allowed by Inder Gill to move on 8 December after obtaining clearance from Manekshaw. They could not be used for strengthening the thrust across the Brahmaputra at Jamalpur. The 95 Mountain Brigade resumed its advance south of Jamalpur on 12 December. In the meantime, 2 Para was dropped in Madhupur area on 11 December. The drop took place on D plus 7 as planned. As we had air supremacy I had wanted the drop to take place at 0900 hours. Unfortunately, Brig Thomas, the Parachute Brigade Commander, was away with his Brigade, en route to Jessore. His second in command, Col Scudder, wanted to drop at last light. I stressed once again that we had complete air supremacy and that the dropping zone was to be protected by Siddiqui who controlled the area; that the signal detachment under Capt Ghosh of his brigade who had been sent to the zone earlier had signalled all clear and therefore there was no requirement for a last light drop. Further, due to the variety of planes used, the drop was likely to be dispersed and retrieval of equipment at night would be a problem. I also pointed out that the earlier we dropped, the more of the retreating enemy forces we could cut off. At this stage Aurora entered my office and joined the discussion. To my surprise he said that as a paratrooper he agreed with Scudder's views. The discussion continued for sometime. Finally, Aurora and Scudder agreed to a compromise at 1600 hours, thus allowing for a little over an hour of daylight. The drop was satisfactory though dispersed, with no mishaps. The battalion organised itself quickly and accounted for at least 300 enemy troops withdrawing from Mymensingh. Had the drop taken place at

0900 hours the bag would have been far larger. To add to my delight, foreign news agency broadcasts reported that about 5000 paratroopers had been dropped in this area, which further unnerved Lt Gen Niazi at Dacca. In fact, Niazi sent a frantic message to the Chief of General Staff of Pakistan saying:

Enemy heli-dropped approx one brigade south of Narsingdi and landed one para-brigade in Tangail area. Request friends arrive Dacca by air first flight 12 December.

The CBS representative telephoned me on the evening of the drop saying he had seen some 5000 paratroopers at Dum Dum airport and would I confirm it. I replied that I could not confirm or deny it. I explained that there was no censorship and that he could report what he saw. This was indeed a fortunate break. Later, at Dacca, Niazi asked me about 50 Parachute Brigade. He had been led to believe that the whole Brigade, instead of just a battalion, was on the outskirts of Dacca which led him to conclude that he did not have the strength to defend the city. He also stated that once Chandpur fell he knew that the war was lost.

The 95 Mountain Brigade Group, 67 Mountain Brigade and 2 Para and Brig Sant Singh's Bihar Battalion under Headquarters 101 Communication Zone Area advanced south and reached just short of the outskirts of Dacca by 13 December. 'Tiger' Siddiqui together with his well armed force of 20,000 had promised to move with our troops to Dacca but eventually did not.

Crossing of Meghna and Advance to Dacca

The enemy was holding Bhairab Bazar in strength and seemed to be intent on defending it. It was, therefore, decided to contain Bhairab Bazar and cross the Meghna further south. All available helicopters and craft, including local craft, were utilized for the crossing.

The lift commenced at 1530 hours on 9 December. The Mi4 helicopters had ferried elements of a battalion and a section of the Light Regiment across. Of the 14 helicopters, only 7 or 8 were available at a time due to maintenance problems. In the meantime, whatever could be was man-handled up to the river and taken across in country-boats. Again, on 11 December elements of an infantry battalion and two sections of mountain guns, without gun towing vehicles were helicopter lifted to Narsingdi, which was secured on 12 December. The tanks tried to reach Narsingdi along the river but could not make it. No vehicles were able to cross the river either. The troops advanced on foot with any available local transport, using even cycles, hand rickshaws, bullock carts and loaded railway wagons pushed by the local people over the rails. By 13 December, some troops had reached the east bank of the Lakhya river, which was crossed by patrols on 14 December. By 15 December patrols of 57 Mountain Division were approaching Tungi. I asked IV Corps Headquarters to move one 5.5 inch gun across the Meghna so that it could shell the outskirts of Dacca and thus create alarm. Unfortunately, they were unable to do this.

On the night on 14/15 December infantry elements of 23 Mountain Division, which was at Chandpur, had been ferried across the river at Daudkandi. They started to build up at Baidyabazar east of Narayanganj, though they had not been able to ferry across any guns or vehicles.

Efforts from the West

Efforts were on to close in on Dacca from the west also. On 13 December, XXXIII Corps was asked to put 340 Mountain Brigade and one squadron of PT 76 tanks across the Jamuna as the deployment of 5 Mountain Brigade had been delayed by Manekshaw. The 101 Communication Zone Area was ordered to position inland water transport craft at Phulchari by 15 December. A contingency plan to cross a brigade group from II Corps across the Padma at Goalundo Ghat had been prepared. Craft from Farakka that had been moved down to Hardinge Bridge on 5 December were to go to Goalundo Ghat in order to move a force to Dacca. However, the craft were not allowed by II Corps to move down from the Hardinge Bridge.

On 13 December we received a signal from Gen Manekshaw ordering us to immediately capture all the towns in Bangladesh that we had bypassed, all towns were named with the exception of Dacca. These included Dinajpur, Rangpur, Sylhet, Maynamati Cantonment, and also Khulna and Chittagong which had been earmarked as primary objectives in the Army Headquarters operation instruction. Surprisingly, no mention whatsoever had been made of the capture of Dacca. We had reached the outskirts of Dacca and to me it was imperative that we capture Dacca rather than waste our efforts in going back and capturing these towns. Had we done so, our operations would have been bogged down. The only towns we were able to occupy were Jessore and Comilla from which the Pakistanis had withdrawn. In the meantime the Soviets had let us know that they would not veto any further resolutions in the UN and that if a cease fire did come into effect we would not be in an advantageous position. Perhaps it was for this reason that Manekshaw felt at this late stage that we should go back and capture the towns we had by-passed. Unfortunately, to make sure our formations received his order Gen Manekshaw had it copied down to the corps concerned. I spoke to the Corps' Commanders not to take any action on the Army Headquarters signal stating that it was only for their information. Orders for operations should only be acted on if sent by Command Headquarters.

Gen Manekshaw's order of 13 December had many

repercussions. Aurora was very upset. He walked into my office blaming me for not wanting to capture towns, particularly Rangpur and Sylhet, which he had from the beginning been keen to capture. A cease fire at this stage would have been a catastrophe. Except for the occupation of Jessore and Comilla, we held no towns. The capture of Dacca, therefore, was absolutely imperative. It was extremely important also that Niazi agree to surrender at the earliest. We were aware of the calls for cessation of hostilities made by his staff and the efforts of the United Nations representatives, Marc Henri and John Kelly in Dacca to obtain some kind of cease fire. I called Lt Col P C Bhalla, who was in charge of signal interception and asked him to put me through to Niazi by telephone-cum-radio links. He managed to get through despite unintentional jamming of this frequency by the Navy at Calcutta. I explained again to the Pakistanis that the forces outside Dacca were very strong, that if they surrendered they would be treated with dignity and that we would protect ethnic minorities. I pointed out that an uprising of the Mukti Bahini in Dacca was imminent. This would have serious consequences for them. They asked if they would be guaranteed their rights under the Geneva Convention and if the safety of military and para military personnel and ethnic minorities would be protected upon surrender. I replied that we would guarantee these and repeated that if they surrendered they would be treated with the dignity to which soldiers are entitled under the Geneva Convention. They then asked if they would be allowed to keep their personal possessions. I said I would try to ensure that they did. Meanwhile, Brig Adi Sethna and I had been working on a draft instrument of surrender. We studied earlier surrenders but the conditions obtaining and the circumstances in this conflict were quite unique. We had prepared a draft and sent it to Army Headquarters for approval. Meanwhile, there was hectic political activity in the

United Nations. The Indian position was that the military repression in East Pakistan made it impossible for East Pakistan to remain part of Pakistan. On 6 December we officially recognized the Provisional Government of Bangladesh. It was now a nation with its own Government whose representatives had been freely elected. The Soviets supported the Indian stand and so far had vetoed all resolutions that did not link a cease fire with the recognition of the will of the people of East Pakistan

According to the Pakistan Commission of Inquiry headed by Justice Hamdoodur Rehman, had the Soviet resolutions of 5 and 7 December advocating a 'Political settlement in East Pakistan which would have resulted in a cessation of hostilities, been accepted, the Pakistani army in the East might have been saved'. The American stand was somewhat similar to the Chinese. On 6 December George Bush, the then American Ambassador to the United Nations, accused India of aggression and on the same day all American economic aid to India was suspended. This followed the suspension, earlier, of military sales. Bush called for an immediate cease fire and withdrawal of troops to their own side of the border and for the positioning of United Nations observers. This resolution was vetoed by the Soviet Union. The Chinese also introduced a somewhat similar resolution which was subsequently withdrawn. On 8 December, after the Government of India had officially recognized the Provisional Government of Bangladesh, an Argentine resolution in the General Assembly demanding a cease fire and withdrawal of troops was passed by 104 votes to 11, with 10 abstentions. A United States resolution was put to the vote on 13 December and opposed by the Soviet Union. A Polish resolution, presumably backed by the Soviet Union, called for an ·immediate cease fire and troop withdrawals. Such a resolution, if adopted would have been disastrous for India. Fortunately for us Bhutto, on 15 December, tore up his copy

131

of the resolution, denounced the United Nations and stormed out of the session. This ended the consideration of the resolution. These pressures at the United Nations and the indications given by the Soviets that they would be unable in the future to veto other resolutions, resulted in great pressure being put on us to capture as many towns as possible. This could account, to some extent, for Manekshaw's order of 13 December to capture all the towns in Bangladesh with the exception of Dacca whose capture, surely, should have been the ultimate aim.

In the West our military operations were not progressing particularly well. On 6 December Inder Gill asked me to send the 130 mm medium artillery regiments, the regiment of medium tanks, 123 Mountain Brigade and 50 Parachute Brigade less a battalion group to the West. I agreed but suggested that we send the squadron of tanks committed in the Bogra sector later. We had already sent all the air defence artillery.

It is pity that we had no clear strategic aims. In fact there was no considered overall strategy, at least none that had ever been discussed. Earlier, on 15 November, I had written to the Director of Military Operations on overall strategy, pointing out the flawed concepts of some of the operations projected in the Western Theatre. This letter was delivered by hand of Brig Sethna. Inder had put up my letter to Gen Manekshaw who took unkindly to the fact that his plans for West Pakistan were being commented on. Inder told me later that Mankeshaw had written on the letter that he did not wish to learn from Maj Gen Jacob how to command the Indian Army (see Appendix 5).

In order to boost their Army's morale, Pakistani propaganda had been alleging that Chinese and American military support had been promised and would materialize and even the Army had begun to believe it. On the evening

132

of 13 December, Niazi's message to the GHQ in West Pakistan was intercepted, which stated:

Dacca under heavy pressure. Rebels have already surrounded the city. Indians also advancing. Situation serious. Promised assistance must take practical shape by 14 December. Will be effective in Silliguri not NEFA and by engaging enemy air bases.

The 'promised assistance' referred to Chinese and American intervention. The Chinese, in order to create apprehensions in India regarding their intentions, started passing weather data in Tibet to their military stations. The American Military Attache, Col Melvin Holst, stationed at Kathmandu, had reported Soviet and Indian apprehensions of Chinese intervention and had advised accordingly. Col Holst and I had attended the same Advanced Artillery and Missile course of instruction at Fort Sill in 1959/1960. After the war he called on me at Fort William but avoided answering questions on the reports emanating from him regarding the possibility of Chinese intervention. According to Siddiq Salik in his book *Witness to Surrender*, Rawalpindi diverted the Pakistani Army's attention from asking for a cease fire by putting out reports that 'Yellow from the north and White from the south' were going to intervene. Our signal intercept organization picked up these transmissions. We checked with our northern border surveillance observation posts but they reported no signs whatever of Chinese moves. Salik reports that Gen Niazi contacted the Chinese and American diplomatic heads in Dacca but they were not aware of any such intentions on the part of their Governments. The Pakistani Eastern Command again asked for confirmation of Chinese and American support were told to wait for another thirty-six hours, that is, up to 12 December. We intercepted these messages to Rawalpindi which confirmed our belief that both China and America were merely barking and had no intention to bite.

Confusion was caused in Delhi by the reported move of the United States aircraft carrier *Enterprise*, an amphibious assault ship, four guided missile destroyers, a guided missile frigate and a landing craft. The Task Force moved through the Straits of Malacca on the night of 13/14 December. American and British nationals had already been evacuated with our permission from Dacca earlier, on 12 December, by air in three Royal Air Force C130s and one United Nations C130 using a small section of the runway that had not been cratered by our Air Force. The RAF crew reported that they had been fired on by the aircraft of the carrier *Vikrant* but fortunately they had missed. This has been confirmed by Air Chief Marshal P C Lal in his memoirs *My Years with the IAF*. Therefore, the Americans could hardly expect us to believe that this Task Force was meant to evacuate their nationals. It was clear that they intended to create apprehension in Indian minds. Adm Krishnan, in one of our regular telephone conversations, expressed concern regarding the movement of the Task Force but I maintained that I could not see the Americans intervening. I was sure that these movements were meant merely as a cautionary signal to us. In any case, the fleet was too far away to reach the Northern Bay in time. Krishnan was not convinced. He also had apprehensions about another Pakistani submarine of the Daphne class operating in the Bay. Though the Daphne did not have the range he felt that it was possible for it to refuel at sea. Perhaps this accounted for the changes in the plan of the amphibious operation and for the movements of the aircraft carrier *Vikrant* which was to have provided support for the landing at Ukhia on 13/14 December, but eventually did not participate.

Gen Manekshaw's calls for surrender were beginning to have an effect on the Pakistani Eastern Command. Manekshaw initially addressed these calls to Maj Gen Rao Farman Ali, advisor to the Governor of East Pakistan. On

9 December the Governor of East Pakistan, Dr A M Malik, sent a signal to Yahya Khan advocating an immediate cease fire. Yahya Khan replied that he would leave the decision to him and instructed Gen Niazi accordingly. Marc Henri, Assistant Secretary General of the United Nations, was given a proposal embodying five points: immediate cease fire, repatriation of the armed forces of West Pakistan, repatriation of other West Pakistanis desirous of returning, safety of persons settled in East Pakistan since 1947 and guarantees that there would be no reprisals. The Governor, waiting for instructions from Rawalpindi, called a high level meeting for 1200 hours on 14 December at Government House. Lt Col P C Bhalla, in charge of signal intelligence brought me the intercept at 0930 hours. I immediately telephoned Air Vice Marshal Devasher the very competent Senior Air Staff Officer at Eastern Air Command in Shillong. We felt that a disruption of the meeting would spur the Governor to accept the surrender calls. The problem was that we did not know which of the two Government Houses would host the meeting, the new or the old. I felt that it would be the old one as Yahya used to occupy the new one when he visited Dacca. We identified the old Government House from a tourist guide map and decided to attack it. Devasher asked if there were any anti-aircraft guns there. I replied that there were none. Relieved, he said that as there was no air opposition at all it would be a 'piece of cake'. The attack was carried out accurately by our aircraft. Gavin Young, in his book *Worlds Apart,* describes what happened when he went to see John Kelly of the United Nations at the Government House just after the initial air strike. Kelly told Gavin Young that Dr Malik was meeting with his cabinet. Maj Gen Rao Farman Ali was present. Gavin Young and Kelly went to see the Governor. Dr Malik, frightened, asked Kelly 'Should we give up now do you think?' Kelly did not want to commit the United Nations and hedged. Gavin Young then met Dr Malik

who asked him if he should send his family to a hotel. Another air raid started and Malik wrote out his resignation, addressed to Yahya Khan. While the raid was still in progress Malik, a devout Muslim, took off his shoes and socks, carefully washed his feet, spread a white handkerchief over his head, and knelt down in the bunker and said his prayers. That was the end of the last Government of East Pakistan.

Earlier, on the night of 13/14, Niazi spoke to the Pakistani Commander-in-Chief, Gen Hamid requesting him to ask Yahya Khan to expedite a cease fire. On 14 December, Yahya sent a signal to Niazi telling him to take necessary measures to stop the fighting and preserve the lives of the armed forces personnel. Yahya Khan sent this message to Niazi

You have fought a heroic battle against overwhelming odds. The nation is proud of you and the world full of admiration. I have done all that is humanly possible to find an acceptable solution to the problem. You have now reached a stage where further resistance is no longer humanly possibly nor will it serve any useful purpose. It will only lead to a further loss of life and destruction. You should now take all necessary measures to stop the fighting and preserve the lives of armed forces personnel, all those from West Pakistan, and all loyal elements. Meanwhile I have moved the UN to urge India to stop hostilities in East Pakistan forthwith and to guarantee the safety of armed forces and all other people who may be the likely targets of miscreants.

The signal was received by Niazi at 1500 hours Indian Standard Time. Niazi and Farman Ali went to see the United States Consul General, Herbert Spivack. Niazi asked Spivack to negotiate a cease fire with the Indians ensuring the guarantees requested earlier. Spivack replied that he was not in a position to do so but would, however, send a message. Rao Farman Ali drafted the message and handed it to Spivack. The message was drafted on the lines of the earlier cease fire proposals:

To put an end to futher loss of human lives and destruction we are willing to cease fire under honourable conditions:

A. Cease fire and stop all hostilities immediately in East Pakistan.

B. Hand over peacefully the administration of East Pakistan as arranged by the UN.

C. The UN should ensure:

    (1) Safety and security of all Armed Forces personnel of both military and para-military forces of Pakistan pending their return to West Pakistan.

    (2) Safety of all West Pakistan . . . civilians and civil servants, pending their return to West Pakistan.

    (3) Safety of non-locals settled in East Pakistan since 1947.

    (4) Guarantee of no reprisal against those who helped and served the Government and the cause of Pakistan since March 1971.

A copy of this note was delivered to the Governor by Farman Ali in the Intercontinental Hotel.

The message, however, was not sent to India but to Washington. At around 1700 hours on 14 December, a diplomat in one of the consular offices in Calcutta apprised me of Niazi's visit to Spivack regarding what he said were cease fire or surrender proposals. I immediately telephoned Herbert Gordon, the United States Consul General, at Calcutta. He denied any knowledge of the matter. I asked him to recheck. He replied 'Jake, cross my heart, I don't know about this request of Niazi'. I then telephoned Gen Manekshaw and suggested he contact the American Ambassador in Delhi. Manekshaw asked me whether I was sure that the information was correct. I told him that the person who had telephoned me was a responsible official and that I believed him. Meanwhile, I would try to get through to Niazi again. Gen Manekshaw spoke to the American Ambassador who stated that he had no knowledge of any request to Spivack. Apparently, Spivack had sent the message to their Ambassador in Islamabad who in turn sent it to the State Department in Washington. Kissinger later confirmed that the State Department decided to hold on to the message for one more day in order to give the Pakistanis more time to take territory in the west before a cease fire came into effect.

Gen Manekshaw received the message on 15 December. He gave assurances that the safety of Pakistani personnel would be guaranteed provided they surrendered. The Pakistan Eastern Command was to contact Eastern Command, Fort William. The Pakistani Commander-in-Chief signalled Niazi to accept. A cease fire was agreed from 1700 hours of 15 December until 9 a.m. the next day and later extended until 1500 hours. As far as can be ascertained, Yahya agreed to a cease fire, which in fact implied surrender. though, as Hasan Zaheer points out in his book *The Separation of East Pakistan*, the Pakistanis did their best to avoid the use of the word 'surrender'. Later, at Dacca, during the discussions on surrender, Niazi expected the document to be drawn up on the lines of the proposals for a cease fire given by him to Spivack. This would account for his reluctance to accept the draft Instrument of Surrender shown to him later at Dacca.

At 0915 hours on 16 December, Gen Manekshaw spoke to me on the telephone telling me to go to Dacca immediately to organize the surrender so that it formally took place that same evening. I asked him whether the draft surrender document we had sent earlier had been approved. When he evaded the question I asked him to specify the terms on which I would negotiate. He told me not to be difficult and that I knew what to do. He would send instructions to Brig Sethna who would have the typed documents sent with

138

Aurora. I told Manekshaw that I had received a radio message from Niazi inviting me to lunch but that I was not keen to accept. He said he would let me know whether I should accept. I briefed Aurora on the matter and made arrangements to fly to Dacca, asking Air Cmdre Purushottam of Advance Headquarters to accompany me, together with our Col Intelligence, Khara. We took a copy of the draft Instrument of Surrender which had earlier been sent to Delhi for approval.

I briefed Sethna and asked him to arrange for the heli-lift of Indian and foreign correspondents. I told him that in addition to the Army, Air Force and Navy Chiefs of the Commands attending the surrender, he should ensure that Col Osmani and Wing Cmdr Khondkar from the Bangladesh Armed Forces attended. Sethna was to inform all formations of the surrender negotiations that were to be held at Dacca and to make sure that the cease fire was enforced.

As I moved down the steps, on my way to the helipad, I bumped into Mrs Bhanti Aurora. When she mentioned that she would see me at the surrender at Dacca, I thought she was joking. Seeing the amazed look on my face she added 'My place is by the side of my husband.' I rushed back to Aurora's office and asked him if he really intended taking his wife to attend the surrender. He replied that he had obtained Manekshaw's approval. I pointed out that there were reports of fighting in Dacca and that it would be risky for the lady to go there. He retorted that it would be my responsibility to ensure her safety. I realized that there was no point in any further discussion and proceeded with my mission.

When we landed at Jessore to change helicopters, I was handed a message from Army Headquarters informing me that the Government had directed that I accept Niazi's lunch invitation. There was still no confirmation or approval of the draft Instrument of Surrender. We could hear sounds of artillery fire in the distance. As we approached the airfield at

Dacca we noticed a helicopter flying away. There were also 18 Pakistani fighters lined up on the tarmac. We noticed the anti-aircraft guns following the movement of our helicopter. The Air Commodore wanted to turn back but I ordered the pilot to land. I was met by the Chief of Staff of the Pakistani Eastern Command, Brig Baqar Siddiqui. Present also was the United Nations representative at Dacca. He had offered his good offices in negotiating with the Pakistani Army but I had no intention of involving the United Nations as I could see no role for them in this situation. The foreign press corps was also present. I asked Air Cmdre Purushottam to liaise with the Pakistani Air Force to ensure the safe landing of Aurora and his entourage. I kidded him regarding the 18 aircraft on the tarmac which were reported to have been shot down or destroyed. Brig Siddiqui, Col M S Khara and I drove to Niazi's Headquarters. On the way to Niazi's Headquarters, we were stopped by the Mukti Bahini. They were in a very belligerent mood and ready to go on the rampage. Representatives of the international press were with them. I explained to them that the war was over and the surrender of the Pakistani Army would take place on the Race Course. They started shouting and wanted to take over the Pakistani Eastern Command Headquarters and to mete out retribution to Niazi and his staff. Heated words were exchanged. I made it clear that there would have to be a bloodless transfer of power to the Bangladesh Government, whose members would be arriving in Dacca shortly to take over charge. I asked the Mukti Bahini to ensure that law and order was maintained and that there were no reprisals. Since there was a cease fire in force and the Pakistani High Command had agreed to surrender, the provisions of the Geneva Convention would have to be respected. They shouted slogans and threatened to act unilaterally. I told them that we would ensure, that the provisions of the Geneva Convention were honoured. The foreign press reported instead, that I had threatened to shoot them. They then let us pass and we reached the Head-quarters at 1300 hours.

Gen Niazi received me in his office. Present at the discussions were Maj Gen Rao Farman Ali, who dealt with civil affairs, Maj Gen Jamshed, Rear Adm Shariff, the Naval Chief, Air Cmdre Imam, the Air Force Cmdre and Brig Baqar Siddiqui. Maj Gen G C Nagra, who had taken over from Gurbax Gill when he was wounded at Jamalpur, had arrived a little earlier. A day after the cease fire came into effect, Nagra contacted the Pakistani outposts and sent a message to Niazi saying, 'Dear Abdullah, I am at Mirpur Bridge. Send your representative.' Niazi, who was expecting me, was at a loss as to what to make of it, as he was not aware if Nagra had any role in the surrender negotiations. Nagra and his escort, flying a white flag, were received on Niazi's orders, at the Pakistani outpost and escorted by the Pakistanis to Niazi's Headquarters. Nagra and Niazi constantly engaged themselves cracking bawdy jokes in Punjabi. Salik in his book states that he declines to record them as none of them are printable. I told Niazi that sporadic fighting continued in many areas, including Tungi and that he should issue orders to the concerned troops to cease firing. While Niazi issued the instructions, I called Nagra outside and instructed him to get on with his tasks. First, he was to move in sufficient troops to maintain law and order. Then, he was to organize the surrender. I felt that it would be appropriate to have a public surrender in full view of the people of Dacca who had suffered so terribly. Other surrender ceremonies in the past had taken place after due preparation. In this particular case, however, the situation was fluid, resources scant and only two or three hours available in which to negotiate the surrender and to organize the ceremony. We could still hear firing close by. I told Nagra to arrange a guard of honour by the Parachute Regiment and a Pakistani Unit. He was to have a table with two chairs for the signing of the documents. He

141

was also to ensure the protection of the Intercontinental Hotel where United Nations personnel, the Red Cross, members of the East Pakistan Government and foreign residents had taken shelter. I asked him to leave a small escort and a radio detachment for me, as I had to proceed to the airport later to receive the Army Commander. I also told him to organize a protective detachment to be sent to the airport for the Army Commander.

I returned to Niazi's office and Col Khara read out the terms of surrender. There was dead silence in the room, as tears streamed down Niazi's cheeks. The others in the room became fidgety. They had expected the document to be on the lines of the proposals they had handed over on 14 December to Spivack, which envisioned a cease fire and evacuation under arrangements of the UN. Farman Ali objected to surrendering to the Indian and Bangladesh forces. Niazi said that what I was asking him to sign was unconditional surrender. When we were drafting the Instrument of Surrender we had tried to word it in such a manner that it would not be offensive. History has shown that rigid, uncompromising surrender terms have had adverse repercussions in succeeding years. It is also important not to corner the defeated by leaving no room for apparent manoeuvre. There had to be some degree of accommodation despite what has happened earlier. I once again reiterated that as we had informed him earlier, through radio broadcasts and in our teleconversations that they would be treated as soldiers with due dignity and the Geneva Convention would be strictly honoured. Further, we would protect all ethnic minorities. These guarantees and clauses in the Instrument of Surrender are unique and are not found in any other surrender documents. Niazi passed on the document to the others to study. They wanted some changes. I reiterated that the terms were already very generous and leaving them to deliberate, walked out. I chatted with the

Pakistani sentry outside. When I inquired about his home, his family and his welfare, he looked perplexed for a while and then burst out in tears. He said that it was a surprise to him that an Indian Army General was concerned about his welfare when his own officers took little or no interest in such matters. As I returned to the office, Niazi informed me that orders to cease firing had gone out to those who were still resisting and the cease fire was being fully implemented. I asked him if the document was acceptable. He handed it back to me without comment. I took this as acceptance. We then discussed with Niazi the modalities of the surrender. He said he would like the surrender to take place here in his office. I told him that the surrender ceremony would take place on the Race Course. He argued that this was not appropriate. I pointed out that Lt Gen Aurora would be given a guard of honour by detachments of the Indian and Pakistani Armies. After that Aurora and Niazi would sign the documents. Niazi would then surrender his sword. He said he did not have a sword. I then stipulated that he surrender his pistol. He seemed most unhappy but kept silent. I again took this as acceptance. There has been some criticism of the public surrender and the combined guard of honour as well as the simple table set up. As I had no instructions or guidance and had to negotiate the terms in what amounted to obtaining an immediate and unconditional surrender without any time or resources for protocol or ceremonial frills, I acted on my own initiative, and in retrospect I do not regret the modalities adopted. In a time frame of some three hours I had to negotiate the terms of surrender and arrange a proper ceremony. Our troops had yet to enter Dacca and sporadic fighting was still going on in and around the capital. Looking back now I feel that it was indeed a 'very close run thing'. Niazi then asked if his officers and men could keep their personal possessions. He had asked this earlier during telephonic contacts and I had indicated that we would consider his request. He then asked about the security of his men after the surrender, as he was apprehensive of the Mukti Bahini. I assured him that our troops were moving in and hopefully by 18 December they would be in sufficient strength to ensure their protection. He again remarked that the Mukti Bahini were well-armed and asked if his men could retain their weapons until we had sufficient strength to ensure their safety. I told him they could keep their weapons until we could disarm them, which I thought would happen within three or four days. There has been some criticism of our decision not to disarm them immediately, but that could be done only after a sufficient number of our own troops had arrived in Dacca. I was hoping that the documents that were to be brought by Aurora to be signed were as per the draft document that I had shown to them. I went outside to use the radio to pass on this information. Nagra had moved off with his escort and radio detachments, leaving no one behind. I then passed, through the Pakistani Army radio, a message to our Eastern Command that arrangements for the surrender were complete and that I should be informed of the Army Commander's expected time of arrival. No reply was received. Instead of landing at Dacca the Army Commander and his entourage had proceeded to Agartala to collect the IV Corps Commander and Divisional Commanders of the Corps.

I was pacing anxiously outside the Headquarters when Allan Hart of the BBC started filming me. We paced up and down for a few minutes. I was unaware that he had a microphone. Fortunately, I had been restrained in my comments. On my return to his office Niazi asked me to join him at lunch and we walked across to the mess. Gavin Young of the *Observer*, waiting outside, said he too was hungry and asked if he could have lunch. I took him in. I did not feel like eating. The lunch was typical mess fare with roast chicken as the main course. Gavin Young had a scoop—two pages of the *Observer* entitled, 'The Surrender Lunch'. The whole scene looked unreal to me, with the mess silver on display and Pakistani officers lunching and chatting away as if it were a normal peace time mess function. Khara and I stood in one corner with little desire to fraternize or eat.

After lunch, I sent a radio message to Calcutta asking again for Aurora's estimated time of arrival. They had no information. At around 1500 hours I asked Niazi to accompany us to the airport. We went in his car with his pilot jeep in front. Trouble then started. The Mukti Bahini tried to prevent us reaching the airfield. Some of them threw themselves on the bonnet of the car. It was fortunate that Khara, a Sikh, was with us. He stuck out his turbaned head saying that Niazi was a prisoner of the Indian Army and that they should not impede us. Sounds of sporadic small arms firing could still be heard all around. We reached the airfield with difficulty. Just before reaching we stopped a jeep with two Indian paratroopers who appeared to be lost and asked them to accompany us. This was a stroke of luck, and as it turned out, most fortunate for us. I was very worried about Niazi's security at the airfield. The Pakistani Military Police in the pilot jeep were armed with revolvers. Other than the two paratroopers with rifles, there were no Indian troops in sight. I told Khara that as Nagra had not sent anyone, he should try and get hold of some troops, and if possible, some tanks. We knew that IV Corps were trying to swim some tanks across the Meghna on the evening of 15 December. Khara left to see what he could do. A little while later a truck loaded with armed Mukti Bahini arrived at the other side of the runway. A man wearing the badges of the rank of a Major General, followed by an escort of two Mukti Bahini soldiers, approached us. The man was 'Tiger' Siddiqui, whom I placed by descriptions I had of him. I sensed trouble and asked the two paratroopers to shield Niazi. I walked towards Siddiqui. It was imperative that Niazi should live to sign the Instrument of Surrender. I was afraid that Siddiqui may have come to shoot Niazi. I asked Siddiqui politely to leave the airfield but he did not budge. I repeated it again as an order. He was still hesitant. Siddiqui then left grudgingly, crossing the runway to his truck. I shouted to him to get the truck off the airfield. I heaved a sigh of relief when it finally moved off. A little while later Khara returned with a PT 76 tank. Siddiqui, with his 20,000 armed men, was to have marched with our troops on to Dacca, but had not showed up. He did not intercept the retreating Pakistani forces at Tangail and now he had shown up at Dacca airfield for purposes that were unclear to me. A few days later he called the international media, with camera crews, to witness the public bayoneting of people he called traitors. These pictures had wide circulation in the international media.

At around 1630 hours the Army Commander and his entourage arrived in a fleet of five Mi4 and four Alloutte helicopters. Niazi and I went to receive them. The Army Commander accompanied by Mrs Aurora alighted Air Marshal Dewan, Vice Adm Krishnan, Lt Gen Sagat Singh, the Divisional Commanders of IV Corps and Wing Cmdr Khondkar also deplaned. Osmani, however, was not to be seen. Niazi, Lt Gen Aurora and Air Marshal Dewan proceeded to the car. I had planned to travel in this car but I had to make way for Mrs Aurora, who took her place by the side of her husband. The car then drove off. I hitched a ride to the Race Course. Though there had been very little time for preparation, the ceremony went off reasonably well. After inspecting the guard of honour Aurora and Niazi proceeded to the table. The surrender documents brought with Aurora were placed on the table. Niazi glanced through them curiously and signed. Aurora signed. I took a careful look at the documents and was aghast to see the heading—which read 'Instrument of Surrender—To Be Signed at 1631 Hours IST (Indian Standard Time)' I looked at my watch. It showed a time of 1655 hours. Niazi then undid his epaulette and removed his .38 revolver with attached lanyard and handed it over to Aurora. There were tears in his eyes. It was getting dark. The crowd on the Race Course started shouting anti-Niazi and anti-Pakistani slogans and abuses. We were concerned about Niazi's safety, there being hardly any troops available at the Race Course. We senior officers formed a cordon around Niazi and escorted him to an Indian Army jeep. I briefed Sagat Singh regarding disarming of the Pakistanis and maintenance of law and order and the movement of the prisoners of war to India. We then returned to the Dacca airfield to take off for Agartala. While we were waiting, Rear Adm Shariff of Pakistan Navy, who had earlier obtained my permission, came to see off Adm Krishnan. The latter asked him to give him his pistol. Shariff removed it from his holster and handed it to Krishnan. We then took off by helicopter for Agartala.

I wondered about the time of 1631 hours that Manekshaw had specified in advance for the surrender I knew that the Parliament was in session. Manekshaw, for some reason, may have informed the Prime Minister that the surrender would take place at 1631 hours. How he arrived at this time remains a mystery to me. At this specified time Aurora and entourage were about to land at the airfield at Dacca. Siddhartha Shankar Ray, Chief Minister of West Bengal, who was present in Parliament, told me later that members had been anxious to know what was happening. According to Ray, the Ministry of Defence representative there had repeatedly stated that Gen Jacob, who had gone to Dacca to negotiate the surrender, was having lunch. It was ironic that in the midst of these tumultuous events Gen Jacob would be remembered by posterity for enjoying a very long and leisurely lunch!

Unfortunately, Col Osmani could not attend the ceremony. The helicopter sent for him was damaged en route by hostile fire and could not be made serviceable in time. His absence has been misrepresented and was to cause problems later.

I got back to Fort William and went to operations room to send a report on the events of the day. Immediately after, in the early hours of the morning, I returned to my quarters. I had barely stepped in when the bell rang. Nicholas Tomalin of the *Sunday Times* was at the door. He was very upset because he had not been given a place on the helicopters to report on the surrender. I briefed him in detail on the surrender and the strategy of the campaign. His report was widely reproduced in the international press.

Sometime later when I examined the revolver surrendered by Niazi, I realized that the weapon was not Niazi's. It was a normal Army issue .38 revolver. The barrel was choked with muck and apparently had not been cleaned for some considerable time. The lanyard was dirty and frayed in parts. This was not the personal weapon of a Commanding General. More likely, Niazi had taken it from one of his military policemen and surrendered it as his personal weapon. I could not help feeling that in his own way, Niazi had got a little of his own back.

Aftermath of War

In anticipation of the liberation of Bangladesh Civil Affairs Cell had been created at Fort William, consisting of Indian Administrative Service (IAS), Police and other miscellaneous services. There were also available a large number of erstwhile East Pakistani civil servants who had fled to India. The Indian Government was of the view that civil affairs should be run by the Army and Indian civilians. I suggested that the Bengali officers of the civil services and police were more qualified to run the country, particularly during the period of transition. The Indian Army should be withdrawn at the earliest from Bangladesh as the Bangladeshis were quite capable of running their own affairs. Our tasks should be maintenance of law and order and that too for a very limited duration and the restoration of the infrastructure in Bangladesh, particularly surface communications such as roads, railway lines and telecommunication services. The other problem was the movement and rehabilitation of the refugees who had crossed into India.

The transfer of power to the Bangladesh Government was rapid and the Civil Affairs Cell created to run the country soon became redundant. In this short time Brig Samir Sinha and his staff of the Civil Affairs Cell functioned most efficiently until they handed over charge to the Bangladesh Government. The movement of prisoners of war to India also proceeded smoothly.

Gen Niazi and his senior commanders were flown to

149

Calcutta on 20 December and were billeted in Fort William. One of the first things I had to do was to have the surrender documents retyped and resigned by Niazi and Aurora. Niazi did so willingly. I had several sessions interrogating Niazi and his generals. Most of them were convinced that though this was a round they had lost, there would be other rounds when they would settle scores.

On the afternoon of 17 December Aurora walked into my office with a copy of the Delhi edition of the *Times of India.* There was a full page article under the headline 'Architects of Victory'. There were resumes and write ups on Gen Manekshaw, Air Chief Marshal P C Lal, Adm Nanda and Maj Gen Jacob. He was visibly upset at the omission of his name. I assured him, and this was true, that I had nothing to do with it. He then told me that he would henceforth deal directly with the Civil Affairs Organization in Dacca where he proposed to spend most of his time. I told him that the sooner the troops come out of Bangladesh the better, as allegations were already being made regarding their behaviour. A few days later Gen Manekshaw spoke to me on the telephone saying that he had heard rumours of looting of Pakistani Army stores. I replied that these were only rumours. He asked me to repeat what I had heard. I replied that I did not repeat rumours. He then decided to speak to Aurora.

The next day Gen Manekshaw ordered me to go to Dacca to enquire about the rumours of looting. I went to Dacca for the day and spoke to the commanders and staff about the rumours that were reaching Calcutta and Delhi. They denied the allegations. On my return, I reported to Manekshaw the assurances given to me but I kept on advocating the immediate withdrawal of our troops. The longer we stayed on in Bangladesh the more unpopular we were likely to become.

Sheikh Mujib had returned on 10 January 1972 and was keen on keeping Indian troops in Bangladesh for some more time but finally agreed to an early withdrawal, which commenced in March. A farewell ceremonial parade was held. I took this opportunity to visit Dacca and call on Mujib. He was a charming and gracious man. I spent several hours with him and was pleasantly surprised by his informal method of functioning. He repeatedly said 'My people love me and I love my people.' He would directly telephone district officials giving them directions. He was very confident of the future and was held in great respect by his people. Sheikh Mujibur Rehman or 'Bangabandhu' as he was affectionately called by his people, strove for the independence of his country. The Bangladeshi people revere him as the Father of the Nation. He has earned the honour of being considered to be one of the great leaders of our times.

A few days later the Bangladesh Government requested for troops to be stationed the Chittagong Hill Tracts to establish posts from where the Bangladesh Army would be able to control the Chakma tribals. I objected as I felt that this was not in our interests. I was told by the Director of Military Operations, however, that the directions had come from the highest and would have to be complied with. Accordingly, an infantry brigade group was moved into the Chittagong Hill Tracts to construct posts for the Bangladesh Army. With the completion of this task our involvement in Bangladesh came to an end.

With this assignment barely over I was asked in June 1972 to raise a Corps Headquarters in Jammu. However, since I needed a break, I took a short holiday to fish at my favourite beats in Kashmir. On my way to Kashmir I called on Gen Manekshaw at Delhi and discussed the coming Simla talks with him. I urged him to consider the importance of regaining Chhamb which lies across the Munnawar Tawi river. Beyond it there is no obstacle in the plains between the Chenab and Jhelum. The Pakistanis are now entrenched on the south bank of the Munnawar Tawi, which is a formidable obstacle. I felt that the territory we had occupied in Ladakh, about 364 square miles, though several times the area of Chhamb, was of lesser strategic or economic value. But Manekshaw did not agree. Perhaps he was constrained by reports put out that in the west we had done well to occupy several thousand square kilometres mainly in the desert areas of Sind for the loss of only a few hundred in Chhamb. Arithmetically this was correct, but strategically it was an error, the outcome of which will be felt in the years to come.

Unfortunately, Manekshaw had no say in the negotiations at Simla where it appears the decisions were determined by political expediency. It has been reported that Bhutto had agreed that the cease fire line or Line of Control be the basis for the delimitation of the international boundary, but insisted that this not be committed in writing for it would jeopardize his political future. In this context, it may be appropriate to recall a famous Sam Goldwynism: 'A verbal contract is not worth the paper it is written on!'

We had won a decisive victory in the marshes and rice paddies of Bangladesh. We had taken some 93,000 prisoners. Yet, at the negotiating table at Simla we were unable to obtain a permanent settlement of outstanding issues with Pakistan. The advantages gained on the battlefield were frittered away at the Simla Conference.

10. From left: Lt Gen Niazi, Brig Sant Singh, Brig Shabeg Singh and Jacob prior to signing of the Instrument of Surrender

11. The farewell parade at Dacca on 23 March 1972

12. Lt Gen A A K Niazi of Pakistan signs the surrender document as Aurora
right) and Jacob (behind, left) keep a close eye on him

13. Lt Gen Jacob addressing troops of the Eastern Command as Mrs Indira Gandhi, Prime Minister looks on

Dramatis Personae

Gen Sam Manekshaw was the Army Chief at the time of the greatest Indian victory in recent memory. He restored the reputation of the Indian Army after the debacle of 1962 and the indecisive war of 1965. He had stood up for the Army, tolerating no interference from the bureaucracy. He was a man with a commanding personality and could speak and write well. However, Manekshaw's tendency to talk out of turn created problems for him. Lt Gen B M Kaul, who had seen in him a potential rival, in 1962 instigated an enquiry against Manekshaw. The charges were baseless and Manekshaw was exonerated. Throughout this crisis Manekshaw conducted himself with great dignity and remained calm, showing no signs of any stress. He went on, later, to become a very successful Army Chief perhaps the best chief the Indian Army has had, whereas Kaul, together with Krishna Menon, could never live down the debacle of 1962.

Manekshaw did not have much regard for Aurora. For reasons I have never been able to discover, he had little time for Rustomji who was perhaps the best head the BSF had or is likely to have. Rustomji was also held in esteem by the Prime Minister. Manekshaw gained the confidence of Prime Minister Indira Gandhi, with whom he got on extremely well, though he tended to ignore the Defence Minister. Manekshaw was not a very good judge of men and was highly susceptible to flattery. All said and done, however, he fully deserved the promotion to the rank of Field Marshal that a grateful Prime Minister bestowed on him just prior to his retirement.

I myself hold Sam Manekshaw in very high esteem. Despite differences in military assessments, he was always kind, tolerant and considerate to me for which I am forever grateful. He was very popular with the rank and file and was respected by all. He was dedicated to the Army and upheld its dignity. As Army Chief and Chairman of the Chiefs of Staff during the 1971 war, the overall responsibility for operations was his. He bore this responsibility well and has earned the honour he received. Sam can rightly take his place amongst the great leaders of independent India.

Jagjivan Ram, whom Manekshaw tended to bypass, was perhaps the best Defence Minister we have had. He had an excellent grasp of military strategy. He was also an able administrator. It was Jagjivan Ram who made sure that the requirements of the three Services—manpower, weaponry, equipment and infrastructural facilities—were provided, as far as possible.

Lt Gen Jagjit Singh Aurora, the Army Commander, was a robust man with a pleasant personality. He spent much of his time to assist in the organization and later the employment of the Mukti Bahini. Maj Gen Lachhman Singh who commanded 20 Mountain Division during the operations and had served with Aurora before, in his book *Victory in Bangladesh,* has this to say of him:

He was physically tough and professionally knowledgeable. He served long years under Manekshaw and was believed to acquiesce readily to his wishes. He was not regarded in the Army as a commander of any distinction, his reputation being that essentially of a staff officer. During the 1971 operations Aurora undertook frequent visits to the forward areas but failed to win the confidence of most field commanders. His relations with the majority of them were like oil and water and he did not build up his subordinate commanders inspite of their successes in battle.

Despite differences in concepts pertaining to the overall strategy and conduct of operations we got on well and worked together to ensure the successful conclusion of the campaign. He was the Army Commander and as such should be given credit for the success of our operations.

Of the Corps Commanders, Lt Gen Mohan Thapan stood out as a man of principle and conviction. He had professional integrity and was competent. He oversaw the operations of his corps effectively. He was well liked by his staff and subordinate commanders. It was unfortunate that he could not get on with Aurora. They hardly spoke to each other. He was well served by Maj Gen Lachhman Singh who commanded 20 Mountain Division. This Division had to clear some of the heaviest enemy opposition in the campaign. Lachhman Singh secured his objectives as planned.

Lt Gen Sagat Singh had dash and personal courage. His relations with Aurora were initially cordial but later turned sour. He did not get on with all of his divisional commanders. Maj Gens Ben Gonsalves and 'Rocky' Hira and Kishna Rao displayed initiative and were largely responsible for the successes of IV Corps whose offensive was swift and well executed. Over all credit for this must also be given to Lt Gen Sagat Singh who was the driving force behind the IV Corps offensive.

Lt Gen 'Tappy' Raina commanded II Corps. He was a quiet, likeable officer who got on well with Aurora but unfortunately had little control over his divisional commanders, one of whom quite openly flouted his orders. Raina was later to become Chief of the Army Staff in which position he conducted himself with competence and dignity.

Maj Gen Gurbax Singh Gill was commanding 101 Communication Zone. He had drive and the courage of his convictions. When Army Headquarters finally refused to allot troops and a headquarters to command our thrust to Dacca, we put Gurbax Singh in command. Gurbax was a fine soldier, down to earth. It is a pity that neither the Army Commander nor the Army Chief were well disposed towards him.

Maj Gen Inder Gill took over as Director of Military Operations at Army Headquarters in August 1971. Inder had enlisted in the British Army early in World War II and had been commissioned in the Royal Engineers. He was awarded the Military Cross for gallantry in a paradrop operations in Greece.

Inder Gill was an officer of a very high calibre, practical, competent and down to earth. He had the courage of his convictions, was not afraid to take decisions and could shoulder responsibility. Inder stood out head and shoulders above the other staff officers at Army Headquarters. He played a pivotal role in the operations, both in the Western and Eastern Theatres, for which he should be given due recognition.

Indira Gandhi was Prime Minister during the critical period prior to and during the operations for the liberation of Bangaldesh. She realized from the very beginning that intervention was inevitable. As there was no National Security Council, no Chief of Defence Staff and no effective coordination of the various intelligence agencies, she was perforce obliged to seek advice from the heads of various agencies and her personal advisors. She accepted Eastern Command's assessment, conveyed through Gen Manekshaw, that the launching of an immediate offensive was impractical and that any offensive should only be launched after due preparation.

Indira Gandhi was pragmatic, determined and courageous. She stood up to Nixon and the pressures from the United Nations. To counter American and Chinese support for Pakistan, she had D P Dhar negotiate a Treaty of Friendship with the Soviets, thus giving us freedom of action. She led the nation to its greatest military victory, restoring our prestige and raising India's status to that of a regional superpower. The liberation of Bangladesh was Indira Gandhi's finest hour.

156

Lessons

In a short war of thirteen days, the Indian and Bangladesh forces liberated approximately 150,000 square kilometres of territory. It was a total victory over a formidable, well-trained army, fighting in difficult terrain suited to the defender. The actual superiority in the field was 1.8 to 1 in our favour, well below the 3 to 1 ratio that strategists consider essential for any offensive.

The estimated casualties, both killed and wounded, of the Pakistani forces in the Eastern Theatre were around 8,000. This estimate is based on the total strength of the Pakistani regular and para-military personnel, as well as attached police elements, given to me by the Chief of Staff, Pakistani Eastern Command as 93,000 of whom approximately 3,000 prisoners of war were taken during the period of fighting. During the campaign the major items of Pakistani arms and equipment destroyed/captured included 41 tanks, 50 guns/ heavy mortars, 104 recoilless guns, 18 F86 aircraft lined up at the Dacca airport and a large number of water craft. Our total casualties were 1,421 killed, 4058 wounded and 56 missing, presumed killed. Of our tanks 24 were destroyed and 13 damaged. Our aircraft losses were 14. The official Pakistani casualities given out for the 1971 operations in the East were 115 officers, 40 junior commissioned officers and 1182 other ranks, whilst in the West the figures given were 70 officers, 59 junior commissioned officers and 1482 other ranks. According to our assessment Pakistani casualities in the East

157

between 26 March and 3 December were: 4500 killed and 4000 wounded; from 4 to 16 December there were 2261 killed and 4000 wounded, the total being 6761 killed and 8000 wounded. The Pakistani Army in the East fought with courage and determination from their defensive positions, where for the most part they remained. They did not expect our bypassing strategy using subsidiary roads and tracks and were taken by surprise by our rapid advances.

Credit for the success of Eastern Command's lightning offensive must go to all ranks of the Eastern Army. They fought with great valour to achieve this decisive victory in a terrain intersected by numerous rivers, against a well organized and determined enemy in a campaign lasting barely thirteen days. Due credit must also be given to the Mukti Bahini. Their guerrilla operations isolated the Pakistanis, hampered their movement and were largely responsible for lowering their morale. Their contribution to the victory of the joint Indo-Bangladesh Forces was therefore enormous.

Credit must go to the general and administrative staffs at all levels who planned the campaign and built up the infrastructure and logistics for the offensive. The superb performance of the Engineers must be commended. Despite the very late release of mainly obsolescent World War II vintage bridging, they were able to collect it from various depots, have it repaired, move it to the launching areas and finally construct the bridges, thus enabling the troops to move and fight.

There are many lessons to be learnt from the operations of 1971. First, for any campaign to be successful it is imperative that the aim or mission be spelt out clearly. Only when clear directives regarding the aim are given, can objectives be selected. This was not the case in 1971. Army Headquarters' aim and presumably the aim given by the Government was to liberate as much territory as possible to set up a

Provisional Bangladesh Government. The importance of Dacca, the final objective, was not even considered by the Chiefs of Staff at Delhi. They were more concerned with the capture of towns and territory. The capture of towns is time consuming and costly in lives. At Command Headquarters the General Staff, with the backing of Inder Gill, selected Dacca as the final objective and Pakistani command and communication centres as subsidiary objectives because they would facilitate our approach to the capital. Our strategy at Command Headquarters was to draw the enemy to the border and commit them to the defence of towns and then bypass those towns by using subsidiary axes. The axes of maintenance could be opened later.

Manekshaw's strategy, endorsed by Aurora, however, was designed to capture maximum territory to include what he termed the 'entry' ports of Khulna and Chittagong. *Dacca was not on his agenda.* Later, on 13 December, when we were on the outskirts of Dacca he issued orders to capture all the towns in Bangladesh that we had bypassed. *Dacca was still not included in this list.* Perhaps Manekshaw felt that we should take as many towns as possible in case the Security Council imposed a cease fire.

Throughout the war Manekshaw apprehensive that the Chinese were likely to intervene, kept 6 Mountain Division, located in North Bengal, in reserve for the defence of Bhutan despite of our repeated requests for its employment for the Dacca thrust. Since we could not employ 6 Mountain Division, we moved three brigades down from the Chinese border, two of these to reinforce troops already earmarked for the Dacca thrust. When Manekshaw got to know of these moves on 30 November, he ordered these brigades back to their original locations. It was not until 8 December, after repeated requests, that he agreed to the employment of two brigades. The third had been ordered earlier to move to the Western Theatre. Had we initially been allotted 6 Mountain

Division or even later, if the employment of two brigades had not been delayed till 8 December, we would have reached Dacca much earlier. In all fairness to Manekshaw the Soviets, the Americans, the American military attache in Kathmandu and some of our foreign affairs and intelligence experts did not rule out Chinese intervention in support of Pakistan. Manekshaw's perforce had to give due weightage to their views.

In no complicated campaign can operations be planned to the last detail and to the final objective. Detailed planning is feasible only up to a certain stage, after which contingency plans should be made. Detailed plans were thus made up to the major rivers in the vicinity of Dacca and contingency plans prepared to supplement the thrust to Dacca from the north.

The absence of a National Security Council to formulate and coordinate political, economic, and foreign policy and military strategies was felt greatly. Intelligence is another sphere that needs to be rationalized. In 1971 the only reliable intelligence we were able to obtain was through signal intercepts by the Signal Intercept Unit of the Army Corps of Signals. The ability to assess is the most critical factor in the area of intelligence. The intelligence agencies, the External Affairs pundits and the Chiefs of Staff were unable to correctly assess and evaluate the emerging Chinese and American positions prior to and during hostilities.

There is no suitable machinery for the direction of war at the highest level. There is no effective Chiefs of Staff organizaiion, nor a Chief of Defence Staff. Air Chief Marshal P C Lal in *My Years with the IAF* writes:

Here I must clarify one doubt that has existed in my mind and also in the minds of others as to what the objectives of the 1971 war were. As defined by the Chiefs of Staff and by each respective service Chief, it was to gain as much ground as possible in the East to neutralize the Pakistani forces there to the extent we could and

160

to establish a base as it were for a possible state in Bangladesh. The possibility that Pakistani Forces in East Pakistan would collapse altogether as they did and that Dacca would fall and that the whole would be available to the leaders of the freedom movement in East Pakistan was not considered something that was likely to happen. Caution demanded that people commanding in the East should work to limited objectives but to go about achieving them as rapidly as possible. It was feared that a delay of even two or three weeks would inevitably bring in the UN Security Council and compel the two sides to come to some sort of cease fire such as Kashmir. With that basic understanding between the three Services, the Army, the Navy, and the Air Force, they were then left to plan their activities as they thought best.

These remarks of P C Lal who was known for his professional integrity, clearly indicate that there was no 'clear political aim' nor was there any agreed strategy or coordinated control of operations by the Chiefs of Staff in Delhi.

The study of military strategy for the most part, had been ignored. Our Staff College and College of Combat taught tactics and staff duties at brigade and divisional levels but no comprehensive strategic studies were undertaken at Service Headquarters and little importance was given to strategic assessments in the event of national security contingencies. Tactics may win battles but it is strategy which wins wars. It is imperative that the study of military strategy is given due importance. It may be noted that though the Americans won all the battles in Vietnam, they did not win that war.

Perhaps the most important lesson of 1971 has been the realisation of the importance of the building up of the infrastructure and logistics required to conduct a campaign. In April the infrastructure was practically nonexistent, especially the road and rail communications to Tripura. Although we did not receive Army Headquarters operation instruction until 16 August, we started building up the infrastructure and logistical back-up for one corps in Tripura in mid May. Had we waited for orders we would not have been able to sustain operations when full-scale hostilities broke out. We took calculated risks in moving equipment and stores on the basis of our concept of the impending operations. Once war was declared almost everything was in place. This, more than any other factor, was the key to our decisive campaign in the East.

1971 also taught us the rewards of close cooperation between the Army, Navy and Air Force. Fortunately, the commanders and staff of the Army, Navy and Air Force commands in the Eastern Theatre worked together in a spirit of cooperation and understanding. The Army, Navy and Air Force commands in the East executed their allotted tasks with great competence.

The 1971 operations brought out our lack of capability in launching amphibious operations. With a coastline of 7600 kilometres, 500 islands and offshore hydrocarbon installations, it is necessary to have well trained and well equipped forces to mount and launch amphibious operations when required. This lesson hopefully has been learnt and attention is now being paid to amphibious warfare.

The need to gain international support is vital in the preparatory stages and subsequent military operations. In March 1971 international support for the independence of Bangladesh was lukewarm. It was imperative that the international press should highlight the atrocities being committed, in order to build up support for an independent Bangladesh. There were a large number of foreign correspondents from the major western newspaper agencies and electronic media. The briefing of these correspondents was done informally by the Chief of Staff. Initially these correspondents were not convinced of the atrocities being perpetrated by the Pakistanis. With the passage of time however, their coverage became totally sympathetic to the cause of Bangladeshi freedom. The contribution of the foreign press and electronic media to the struggle for Bangladesh's independence should be given due weightage. Unfortunately, today this lesson from the 1971 war has been forgotten. The handling of foreign correspondents and the international electronic media leaves much to be desired and India's viewpoint on critical matters does not receive due attention.

Reflections

I look back on the thirty-seven years I spent in the Indian Army, with its ups and downs, as the happiest and most enjoyable period of my life. As a young officer in command of a troop and later, a battery in World War II, I realized early on that if one was proficient one could stand tall despite ingrained prejudices. Though on the whole the British officers I worked with dealt fairly with me, occasionally I had to counter prejudice in being an Indian in an army that was then almost entirely officered by the British. British commanders respected professional competence and I was given command of a battery during operations, superceding many British officers in the regiment. I was lucky to be given command and responsibility at a very early age. I learned to appreciate the problems of mobile warfare in desert terrain as well as the importance of mobility and manoeuver in the mountains and jungles of the Arakan. I was fortunate to have had the opportunity of taking part in various amphibious operations down the Arakan coast and low-intensity and counter-insurgency operations in Sumatra. Perhaps the most valuable lesson that was brought home to me was the importance of the management and handling of men. Very early on in my service I learnt how necessary it was to look after the interests of my men. During lulls in operations in the Arakan I remember making trips to the accounts section of the Field Artillery Training Centre at Mathura to go through each man's pay accounts in order to ensure that all dues had been credited. As a troop commander and later as a battery commander I knew each man personally and was familiar with the details of his village and family background. Unfortunately, today man management is not given the importance it deserves.

The motivations of today are different. The majority of today's officer intake, prior to commissioning, opts for services such as the Army Service Corps and the Army Ordnance Corps. Few opt for the combat arms, the Armoured Corps, Infantry and Artillery. Their outlook, too, is different perhaps due to the rapidly changing social environment. The young officer of today plans his economic future with meticulous detail. The officer's wife plays a more important role than ever before. A parallel chain of command appears to have emerged from the very top, right down to the unit commander's wife. This chain of command created under the guise of welfare influences many other areas in which it should have no say.

When I joined the Army, the Service Officer had a dignified status and his equation with the Indian Civil Service and the Police was well established. With the passage of time this equation has been steadily eroded. The equation of the Service Officer with the Civil Service and Police cadres has been degraded several steps. It has been further complicated by the large-scale proliferation of higher ranks in the Army for 'career' incentives to keep up with the rank and status of the Indian Administrative Service and the Police. The dignity of the armed forces, too, is being steadily eroded. This, compared with the more lucrative emoluments in business, has led to a lack of suitable officer intake, resulting in a critical shortage of junior and middle rank officers.

The bureaucracy in olive green runs the Army from South Block and Sena Bhawan. Army Headquarters remains top heavy and overstaffed and the proliferation of higher ranks means that slots that were held by majors and lieutenant colonels are now being filled by brigadiers and major generals. The Whitehall system inherited from the British is today more Whitehall than Whitehall itself. Financial approvals and the enhanced power of civilians in the Defence Ministry stifle initiative and slow down decision making. Civilian control of the armed forces is being misconstrued by the bureaucracy to mean civil service control. The authority of the Service Chiefs, too, has been marginalized. The Defence Secretary and his civil service subordinates in the ministry wield power at the expense of the Service Chiefs and General and Administrative Staffs. Some of the responsibility for lowering the status of the Service Chiefs must be placed on the Service Chiefs themselves as inter-service rivalries are exploited by the civil service who tend to play one Service against another. Successive governments have failed to appoint a Chief of Defence Staff and a viable machinery for the coordination of the Chiefs of Staff Committee has been resisted because of the fear that a strong Chief of Defence Staff may be tempted to stage a coup. These fears in the Indian environment are without foundation. The Indian Army is based on a diverse ethnic structure and its leadership, too, is drawn from all regions and religions. This is very unlike the structure of the armed forces of Pakistan, which is predominantly Punjabi.

There is a tendency among some senior army officers to curry political favour. One Army Commander gave a press release praising the political party in power and criticizing an opposition-governed state administration and was promoted to Chief of the Army Staff superceding a senior colleague. An important criterion for selection of service chiefs appears to be amenability. There are cases where military assessments are made to suit a political policy. One example is the ill planned intervention in Sri Lanka. The operation was mounted hastily, largely based on the assessment of a very senior General that he could conclude the operations in

seven days! Launched without any proper military assessment based on reliable intelligence, the operation committed
troops piecemeal resulting in heavy casualties, and finally
withdrawl.

Our Army, Navy and Air Force have always carried out
their duties under difficult conditions with dedication and
competence. The nation should be proud of them. They
require to be suitably equipped in order to ensure the
defence of the country. They also deserve to have better pay,
emoluments and other facilities commensurate with the
responsible roles they have to perform. Armed Forces that
have been neglected in peace cannot be revived overnight
in times of danger so that they can effectively counter the
threats that emerge. Modern weapon systems require skills
that take a considerable time to acquire and master. Defence
has not been given the priority it requires. The Government
must reassess the potential threats that arise from the
unstable and volatile geomilitary environment that obtains
today and is likely to continue into the next decade and
make the necessary appropriations to ensure that the Armed
Forces have the wherewithal to defend the country.

The rifle and helmet that forms the centre-piece of the Amar Jawan War Memorial at New Delhi's India Gate once belonged to a soldier, unknown to history, who died on the battlefield on the outskirts of Jessore. There is no inscription on this memorial.

There is an inscription chiselled into the living rock in the War Memorial at Kohima for those who fell in that World War II battle. It reads:

> *When you go home*
> *Tell them of us and say*
> *For your tomorrow*
> *We gave our today.*

Similar sentiments had been expressed much earlier for those Spartans who had fallen at Thermopolaye. They are equally appropriate for our jawans who laid down their lives in the rice paddies of Bangladesh. Let us not forget them.

Questionaire sent by Field Marshal S H F J Manekshaw on 8 March 1978 and Reply by Lt Gen J F R Jacob

1. The operational considerations in the planning of the war in 1971 with respect to:

   (*a*) The required force levels.
   (*b*) The use of naval and air power.
   (*c*) The intelligence capabilities of our forces.
   (*d*) The time-table to achieve the overall victory.

2. The ingredients that made for success in the operations, e.g. a clear political aim, excellent inter-service cooperation, motivated and well-trained commanders and troops.

3. The Indo-Pakistani war of 1971 has been referred to as the Engineer's war, in that the Indian Army Engineers had to put up 10,000 feet of bridging in the campaign. There was the problem of crossing amphibious vehicles, swift flowing rivers, many rivers and canals, muddy bank and limited axes necessitating helicopter 'air-bridging'. What importance did this aspect play in the planning and eventually the direction of war? How did we ensure sufficient bridging for the Army at the required time and place and how were the main troops trained to operate with the equipment?

4. To what extent did the Civil and military intelligence have access to tactical and strategically intelligence before and during the war. The role played by the Mukti Bahini, prior to actual operations, during the operations both with regard to intelligence and actual fighting. Did the civil population assist in obtaining and giving intelligence to our forces?

5. Did close air support provide a major contribution to tactical battles and if so how was this coordinated and executed?

6. To what extent would you describe the importance of junior commanders and NCOs in the command and control of troops in battle?

FM S H F J Manekshaw, MC
8 March 1978

I sent the following reply to Manekshaw's queries:

1. The operational considerations in the planning of the war in 1971 with respect to:

(a) *The required force levels.* The forces provided were adequate for the regional tasks allotted by Army Headquarters. However, the initial allotment and deployment made was based on the objectives spelt out by Army Headquarters in their Operation Instruction of August 1971, which, in effect, boiled down to (i) capture of the 'entry ports of Khulna and Chittagong' and (ii) seizing maximum territory.

You may recall that there were sharp exchanges in the Operations Room between your DMO, KK and self regarding objectives, particularly the phrase 'that the main thrust would be weighted towards Khulna'. I had pointed out then that these two ports were not the major consideration due to the impending naval blockade, and that the geo-political heart was Dacca. In the initial deployment the force level for the northern thrust was therefore inadequate. You are well aware of the efforts we later made to employ troops allotted to the China border for this purpose.

(b) *The use of naval and air power.* As visualized, considering the resources available to Pakistan, the tasks spelt out to the Navy and the Air Force were respectively a naval blockade and creation of a favourable air situation in support of the Army.

These were carried out effectively as the enemy had very restricted naval and air elements in the theatre. As far his air power was concerned, no great air action took place and the Air Force quite rightly concentrated on the only airfield for their fighters, Dacca, and put it out of action, after which there was no air interference. The naval blockade was successful due to the lack of ability of Pakistan to deploy naval forces in this area.

(c) *The intelligence capabilities of our forces.* The only effective intelligence we had was Signal Intelligence (SI). The equipment used was obsolete and haphazardly deployed. Further, it was controlled by the Director of Military Intelligence (DMI). The DF (direction finding) equipment was unable to get any accurate fixations. You may recall that, as a result of my personal request to you, you placed SI directly under Eastern Command. Despite limitations of equipment we were able to redeploy the equipment and thus were able to build a fairly accurate picture of Pak deployment and strengths. In fact, it was the only reliable means we had. We also started code-breaking but only managed to break the naval code.

(d) *The time-table to achieve the overall victory.* I am not clear regarding 'the time-table' and what you mean by 'achieve overall victory'. The concept of total victory was only evolved by Army Headquarters just prior to hostilities. To the best of my knowledge no fixed time-table was ever laid down. We in Eastern Command were initially working on a three weeks time-frame. We had hoped that with some luck it could be speeded up.

2. The ingredient that made for success in the operations, e.g. a clear political aim, excellent inter-service cooperation, motivated and well trained commanders and troops.

(a) *Clear aim.* What was the political aim? If the political aim was the independence of Bangladesh, that meant the occupation of the whole country including Dacca. If this was clear, then why was not the military part spelt

171

out in the Operation Instruction of August, and not just
prior to the onset of hostilities? Though nothing directly
was spelt out, the political aim was, I think, establishment of a Bangladesh Government in liberated territory.
Once established this Government was to be recognized. You may recall that this was attempted in the
Mymensingh area, and when it failed the emphasis was
shifted to the east. Was there then a clear political aim?

(b) *Inter-Service Cooperation*. This was good at Command
level.

(c) *Motivated and well-trained commanders and troops*.
Yes.

3. The Indo-Pakistani war of 1971 has been referred to as the
Engineer's war, in that the Indian Army Engineers had to put
up 10,000 feet of bridging in the campaign. There was the
problem of crossing amphibious vehicles, swift flowing
rivers, many rivers and canals, muddy banks and limited
axes necessitating helicopter 'air-bridging'. What important
role did this aspect play in the planning and eventually the
direction of war? How did we ensure sufficient bridging for
the Army at the required time and place and how were the
main troops trained to operate with this equipment?

It will be more correct to say that it was a war of manoeuvre.
The role of the Engineers in war is to help the Army move
and fight. Bridging was only one such problem. The
strategic considerations, particularly the selection of
objectives and the thrust-line for these objectives were
communications and control centres in depth in rear of
defended localities. The Fortress deployment of troops by
Gen Niazi were by-passed and left alone. This meant that
the axis of advance should avoid major opposition, as
almost all the road axes were defended. The opening of an
axis of maintenance was subsequent. That was the pattern
throughout our operations. In other words, an axis of
advance and axis of maintenance need not necessarily

be the same. Advances can be made using *kutcha* (dirt) tracks until such time as a suitable maintenance axis is opened.

Heli-lift

Helicopter lift was part of our mobility. Unfortunately, the Mi8s promised did not came in time and the heli-lift was restricted to the limited number of Mi4s.

Bridging

Army Headquarters were slow in releasing bridging and, when eventually it was released by K K Singh the DMO before his departure in August, it was a matter of touch and go to collect bridging from depots, have it repaired and moved it to its locations. In fact, the last bridge reached its location early December and at the end of the war we had no reserves and every single foot of bridging had been laid. Major problems lay in the movement of this bridging across kutcha tracks and the construction of approaches and exits. We also resorted to large scale ferrying with our own and local resources.

4. To what extent did the Civil and Military Intelligence have access to tactical and strategically intelligence before and during the war? The role played by the Mukti Bahini, prior to actual operations, during the operations both with regard to intelligence and actual fighting. Did the civil population assist in obtaining and giving intelligence to our forces?

Again, if my memory serves me right, throughout the period before the war we received two half-pages from RAW on intelligence. The main information was built up by Signal Intelligence.

Mukti Bahini

Guerrilla operations take a considerable time to organize. The infrastructure for these operations must be carefully laid out in the interior and the insurgency cells built up over a period of time. In training an insurgent force, it is necessary that leaders are specially selected and given intensive training. Without dedicated and trained leadership insurgency operations are likely to founder.

The emphasis in training in Operation Jackpot was on quantity rather than quality. The large number of semi-trained guerrillas without effective junior leadership did not produce results commensurate with their numbers. Special emphasis should have been given to the selection of leaders and their training.

The achievements of the Bangladesh forces and guerrillas did not entirely come upto our expectations. However, despite the limitations of training and leadership they still achieved very tangible results. Their contribution to the defeat of the Pakistani Army was enormous, e.g.

(*a*) Occupation of areas in the interior.

(*b*) Lowering of the morale of the Pakistani Army due to the creation of a hostile environment, restricting their movements and confining them to their bases.

5. Did close air support provide a major contribution to tactical battles and if so how was this coordinated and executed.

Air Support

Due to the fast moving battles and our by-passing tactics we used air support mainly for interdiction, isolation of the battlefield, and prevention of movement along the rivers back to Dacca. Close air support for ground targets was almost negligible. However, the interdiction effort was very credible. It was due to our persuasion that the Gnats were used in the interdiction role with reasonable success. Our major problem was full utilization of unexpended sorties due to the fast moving nature of operations. However, we were able to get maximum results by switching sorties from one sector to another.

6. To what extent would you describe the importance of junior commanders and NCOs in the command and control of troops in battle?

In general junior officers and NCOs performed well and showed dash and elan. However, JCOs sometimes gave the impression of being cautious.

APPENDIX 2

INSTRUMENT OF SURRENDER SIGNED AT DACCA AT *1631* HOURS (IST)

ON 16 DEC 1971

The PAKISTAN Eastern Command agree to surrender all PAKISTAN Armed Forces in BANGLA DESH to Lieutenant-General JAGJIT SINGH AURORA, General Officer Commanding in Chief of the Indian and BANGLA DESH forces in the Eastern Theatre. This surrender includes all PAKISTAN land, air and naval forces as also all para-military forces and civil armed forces. The forces will lay down their arms and surrender at the places where they are currently located to the nearest regular troops under the command of Lieutenant-General JAGJIT SINGH AURORA.

The PAKISTAN Eastern Command shall come under the orders of Lieutenant-General JAGJIT SINGH AURORA as soon as this instrument has been signed. Disobedience of orders will be regarded as a breach of the surrender terms and will be dealt with in accordance with the accepted laws and usages of war. The decision of Lieutenant-General JAGJIT SINGH AURORA will be final, should any doubt arise as to the meaning or interpretation of the surrender terms.

Lieutenant-General JAGJIT SINGH AURORA gives a solemn assurance that personnel who surrender shall be treated with dignity and respect that soldiers are entitled to in accordance with the provisions of the GENEVA Convention and guarantees the safety and well-being of all PAKISTAN military and para-military forces who surrender. Protection will be provided to foreign nationals, ethnic minorities and personnel of WEST PAKISTAN origin by the forces under the command of Lieutenant-General JAGJIT SINGH AURORA.

(JAGJIT SINGH AURORA)
Lieutenant-General
General Officer Commanding in Chief
Indian and BANGLA DESH Forces in the
Eastern Theatre

16 December 1971.

(AMIR ABDULLAH KHAN NIAZI)
Lieutenant-General
Martial Law Administrator Zone B and
Commander Eastern Command (PAKISTAN)

16 December 1971.

APPENDIX 3

To Brigadier H S Kler

Brigade Commander
95 Mountain Brigade
Jamalpur
091735 Dec

Dear Brig,

Hope this finds you in high spirits. Thanks for the letter.

We here in Jamalpur are waiting for the fight to commence. It has not started yet. So lets not talk and start it.

40 sorties, I may point out are inadequate. Please ask for many more.

Your remark about your messenger being given proper treatment was superfluous. Shows how you underestimate my boys. I hope he liked his tea.

Give my love to the Muktis.

Hoping to find you with a sten in your hand next time, instead of the pen you seem to have so much mastery over.

I am, your most sincerely
[Col Sultan]
Comd Jamalpur Fortress

Lt Col A K Philip
Commanding Officer

235, Yantrik Jalparivahan
Parichalan Company Engineers
235 IWT, Op Coy Engineers
Alambazar, Calcutta
01 Jan. 87

My dear General,

The move of IWT vessels ex-Calcutta as well as ex-Patna were completed during July 71. The IWT vessels were concentrated downstream of the Farakka Barrage till hostilities were declared. The IWT Task Force was to move down the Ganges and carry on board infantry and armour on reaching Hardinge bridge. I have ascertained from some of the JCO's who were part of the Task Force that they reached the Hardinge bridge on 05 Dec. 71 and that the IWT Task Force did not get any orders for their move forward to Faridpur till the cease-fire was declared. However, the unit was asked to proceed to Dacca on 18 Dec. 71, which they did and carried 'on board' returning prisoners of war.

With warm regards and best wishes,

A K Philip

Lt Gen J F R Jacob

APPENDIX 5

Personal

Maj Gen J F R Jacob   Headquarters Eastern Command
Chief of Staff   Fort William
                                                                 Calcutta
                                                              15 Nov. 71
My dear Inder,

1. This concerns overall strategy in the event of a war with Pakistan. In the East conditions are ripe for a swift offensive and I have no doubt that if so required our aim will be fulfilled in a short time. I will say no more about this aspect.

2. In the West, the conditions are different. You are faced with a well equipped force strong in armour. Further, by extensive fortification and construction of obstacles advances will be both difficult and costly. We have seen here that where properly constructed defences are manned these take a long time to reduce and at great cost. I presume that we have constructed defences on our side of the border. With current the deployment on both sides, there is little scope for strategical surprise as strengths and locations of opposing forces are well known to each other.

3. In view ·of the above, I feel that in the event of war a swift offensive is launched in the East and a holding action takes place in the West. Pakistani forces in the West should be made to lauch attacks on our prepared positions and maximum attrition imposed on them. As and when this attrition becomes sizable and when a large proportion of his armour has been destroyed, we can regroup for offensives, the main one being the geostrategical heart of Pakistan, i.e. Multan. On completion of our tasks in the East we would be in a position to move sizeable forces to the West for an offensive if so required.

179

4. In my study of the initial concentration of Pakistani forces, it would appear that the Shakargarh bulge is being prepared to draw in our own troops. There is also a sizable concentration on the Southern flank which could aim for the Hissar Road or Bikaner. I am sure you must also have taken this into consideration.

5. At the risk of repetition we should not be concerned with holding on to territory particularly in the desert. The terrain there should be used to draw in Pakistani forces over bad terrain and difficult communications where they can be dealt with on ground of our choosing. In the Western sector I feel that we are planning to attack in line all along the front. Thus our concentration is being dissipated and no single thrust is, therefore, sufficiently weighted. What bearing have minor thrusts from Rajasthan on the overall situation? We should hold in certain unimportant sectors even at the cost of letting him occupy trackless wastes and be able to concentrate our forces in areas which are worthwhile and further the overall aim, which in the event of war surely must be the defeat of his Armed Forces.

6. I have spoken to you earlier about the potentialities of the area around Fort Abbas by either side. This is the only open flank that can be profitably used by anyone so desiring.

7. These are my personal views. You can give any weightage to them. If you feel that there is something worthwhile in these suggestions there is still time to make adjustments to your contingency plans.

8. Finally John Bunyan in his preface to the 'Pilgrims Progress' wrote:

> *What is my gold be wrapped*
> *up in ore*
> *who throws away the apple*
> *for the core.*

Sincerely
Jake

Maj Gen I S Gill, PVSM, MC
DMO

Interview given by Gen Sam Manekshaw to Quarterdeck (1996)

During the time of the 1971 war, there were personalities in the War room, such as Adm Nanda and Adm Dawson. Can you recall anything about them in the period leading up to the war, or during the war, which you still remember, or which strikes you as something interesting.

I can tell you before the war started. I can't remember the date now—sometime in April or something like that. There was a cabinet meeting to which I was summoned. Smt Gandhi was terribly angry and terribly upset because refugees were pouring into West Bengal, into Assam and into Tripura.

'Look at this—so many are coming in—there is a telegram from the Chief Minister of Assam, a telegram from...what are you doing about it?' She said to me.

I said, 'Nothing. What has it go to do with me?'

She said, 'Can't you do something? Why don't you do something?'

'What do you want me to do?'

'I want you to march in.'

I said, 'That means war' and she said, 'I don't mind if it is war'.

So I sat down and I said, 'Have you read the Bible?'

Sardar Swaran Singh said, 'What has the Bible got to do with it?'

'In the first book, the first chapter, the first paragraph of the Bible, God said, "Let there be light and there was light"—so you feel that "Let there be war and there is war". Are you ready? I certainly am not ready.'

Then I said, 'I will tell you what is happening. It is now end of April. In a few days time, 15-20 days time, the monsoon will break, and in East Pakistan when it rains the rivers become like oceans. If you stand on one side you can't see the other. I would be confined to the roads. The airforce would not be able to support me, and the Pakistanis would thrash me—that's one.'

'Secondly, my armoured division is in the Babina area; another division, I can't remember which, is in the Secunderabad area. We are now harvesting. I will require every vehicle, every truck, all the road space, all the railway space to move my soldiers and you will not be able to move your crops', and I turned to Shri Fakruddin Ali Ahmed, the Agriculture Minister, and said, 'if there is a famine in India they will blame you. I won't be there to take the blame'.

Then I turned around and said, 'My armoured division which is supposed to be my strike force has got twelve tanks which are operational out of the whole lot.'

Y.B. Chavan asked, 'Sam, why only twelve?'

I said, 'Sir, because you are the Finance Minister. I have been asking, pleading for months. You said you have got no money, that's why'.

Then I said, 'Prime Minister, if in 1962, your father had asked me as the Army Chief and not Gen Thapar and your father had said "Throw the Chinese out", I would have turned around and told him "Look, these are the problems". Now I am telling you what the problems are. If you still want me to go ahead, Prime Minster, I guarantee you 100 per cent defeat. Now, you give me your orders.'

Then Jagjeevan Ram said, '*Sam, maan jao na*'.

I said, 'I have given my professional view, now the Government must take a decision.'

The Prime Minister didn't say anything. She was red in the face and said, '*Achccha, cabinet char baje milenge.*'

Everybody walked out. I being the juniormost was the last to leave and I smiled at her.

'Chief, sit down.'

So I said, 'Prime Minister, before you open your mouth, do you want me to send in my resignation on the grounds of mental health, or physical?'

She said, 'Oh, sit down Sam. Everything you told me, is true?'

'Yes. Look, its my job to fight. It is my job to fight to win. Are you ready? I certainly am not ready. Have you internally got everything ready? Internationally have you got everything ready? I don't think so. I know what you want, but I must do it in my own time and I guarantee you 100 per cent success. But, I want to make it quite clear. There must be one commander. I don't mind, I will work under the BSF, under CRPF, under anybody you like. But I will not have a Soviet telling me what to do and I must have one political master who will give me instructions. I don't want the refugee ministry, home ministry, defence ministry all telling me. Now, make up your mind.'

She said, 'All right Sam, nobody will interfere, you will be in command.'

'Thank you, I guarantee you accomplishment.'

So there is very thin line between becoming a Field Marshal and being dismissed! It could have happened! So that was one incident I can tell you about and you can put it in your own words.

What about the other two Chiefs. When did they come in?

They were not in on the initial meeting, then I had to brief them, I had to tell them about it.

Source: *Quarterdeck*, Directorate of Ex-Servicemen's Affairs, Naval Headquarters, New Delhi, 1996.

APPENDIX 7

Pakistani Forces in East Pakistan

DEPLOYMENT AND LOCATIONS ON COMMENCEMENT OF HOSTILITIES

Formations/Units	Locations
HQ Eastern Command (Lt Gen A A K Niazi)	Dacca
Artillery	
43 Compo LAA Regt	Dacca with elements at Jessore and Comilla
46 LAA Bty	Chittagong
36 Inf Div (Maj Gen Mohd Jamshed Khan)	
HQ	Dacca
93 Inf Bde (Brig Abdul Qadir Khan)	
HQ	Mymensingh
83 Indep Mor Bty	Kamalpur–Mymensingh
33 Punjab	Mymensingh–Phulpur–Kaluaghat
31 Baluch	Jamalpur–Rajendraganj–Hathibanda–Diwanganj–Tangail
70 Wing Rangers	Mymensingh–Kishoreganj
71 Wing Rangers	Jariajhan Jail–Shibganj–Biri Siri–Bijaipur
39 Inf Div (Maj Gen Rahim Khan)	
HQ	Chandpur (was under process of raising, but remained incomplete due to commencement of operations)

53 Fd Regt	Comilla–Feni
53 Inf Bde (Brig Mohd Aslam Niazi)	
HQ	Feni
15 Baluch	Feni area
39 Baluch	Lakshman–Mean Bazar–Chaudagram
23 Punjab	Mean Bazar–Parikot
21 AK Bn	Laksham–Feni
117 Inf Bde (Brig Sheikh Mansoor Hussain Attif)	
HQ	Comilla
Sqn tanks (Chaffees)	Comilla area
30 Punjab	Saldanadi–Bibirbazar
25 FF	Lalmai–Maynamati with element at Laksham
12 AK Bn (Less two coys)	Comilla
91 Inf Bde (Brig Mian Taskin-ud-din)	
HQ (under raising)	Chittagong
24 FF	Ramgarh–Karerhat–Zorarganj–Chittagong
97 Inf Bde (Brig Ata Mohd Khan Malik)	
HQ	Chittagong
48 Baluch (Garrison Battalion)	Chittagong
2 Cdo Bn	Rangamati–Kaptai
60 Wing Rangers	Chittagong–Ramgarh–Karerhat area with one
61 Wing Rangers	coy at Cox's Bazar
14 Inf Div (Maj Gen Qazi Abdul Majid Khan)	
HQ	Ashuganj
31 Fd Regt	Sylhet–Shamshernagar–Brahman Baria
88 Indep Mor Bty	Sylhet
171 Indep Mor Bty	Comilla

202 Inf Bde (Brig Asghar Hussain)
HQ — Sylhet
31 Punjab — Chattak–Sylhet–Jaintiapur–Charkhai

91 Mujahid Bn (less two coys) — Sunamganj–Sheola area
Khyber Rifles ⎤
Thal Scouts ⎬ Mixed with regular Bns and deployed in whole area
Tochi Scouts ⎦
2 Coys ex 12 Akr Bn — Sylhet

313 Inf Bde (Brig Iftikar Rana)
HQ — Maulvi Bazar
22 Baluch — Kalaura–Juri area
30 FF — Srimangal–Shamsher Nagar–Kamalpur area

Two Coys 91 Mujahid Bns — Fenchuganj–Sherpur area
Elements Tochi Scouts — Barlekha area

27 Inf Bde (Brig Sadullah Khan)
HQ — Brahman Baria
Two Tps Tanks (Chaffees) — Akhaura
33 Baluch — Kasba–Saidbad–Kutt

12 FF — Gangasagar–Akhaura Paharpur–Fakirmura area

16 Inf Div (Maj Gen Nazir Hussain Shah)
HQ — Nator (unconfirmed reports of move to Bogra area)

29 CAV less sqn — Thakurgaon–Dinajpur–Ghoraghat–Hilli

48 Fd Regt — Thakurgaon–Hathibanda–Nageshwari area

80 Fd Regt — Khetlal–Hilli
117 Indep Mor Bty — Nageswari–Kurigram

23 Inf Bde (Brig Iqbal Mohd Shafi)
HQ — Saidpur
25 Punjab (was scheduled for relief by 8 Punjab) — Hathibanda–Lalmanirhat Nageshwari–Kurigram

186

26 FF	Dinajpur–Phulsari
48 Punjab	Thakurgaon–Pachagarh
8 Punjab	Lalmanirghat–Rangpur
34 Punjab (Recce and Sp Bn)	Thakurgaon–Boda–Nilphamari
86 Mujahid Bn	Elements at Hathibanda–Hilli–Gaibanda and Rangpur

205 Inf Bde (Brig Tajmmal Hussain Malik)

HQ	Khetlal
32 Baluch	Ghoraghat–Gobindganj
4 FF	Hilli
3 Baluch	Jaipurhat–Jaipur and Muhabbatpur

34 Inf Bde (Brig Mir Abdul Nayeem)

HQ	Nator
32 Punjab	Nawabganj–Shibganj–Rahanpur–Rajshahi
Coy 12 Punjab	Ishurdi
13 FF	Panitala–Rasulbil–Sapahar–Gondardanga

9 Inf Div (Maj Gen M H Ansari)

HQ	Jessore
3 Indep Armed Sqn (Chaffees)	Jessore (Sqn completely eleminated on 22 Nov)
55 Fd Regt	Satkhira (One Bty) and Jhingergacha area (2 Coys)
49 Fd Regt	Meharpur–Chuadanga–Kushtia
211 Indep Mor Bty	Chaugacha

57 Inf Bde (Brig Manzoor Ahmed)

HQ	Jhenida
Sqn 29 CAV	Kushtia–Beramara area
18 Punjab	Meherpur–Chaudanga–Darsana–Natudaha area
50 Punjab	Jhenida–Kotchandpur
29 Baluch	Bheramara–Salimpur Khaliskundi–Kushtia

107 Inf Bde (Brig Malik Hayat Khan)

HQ	Jessore

187

22 FF	Jhingeragacha–Benapole
38 FF	Afra–Sajiali–Asanagar
6 Punjab	Jessore
21 Punjab (Recce and Sp Bn)	Satkhira–Kalaroa–Jessore
15 FF	Jessore
12 Punjab Less Coy	Jessore

SUMMARY

Formations/Units	Total	Remarks
Inf Div Hq	3	Excl one skeleton (HQ 36 Div) and one under raising (HQ 39 Div)
Bde HQ	13	Incl one skeleton (91 Bde)
Inf Bns	35	Incl two AK Bns
Armd Regt (29 Cav)	1	(Chaffees)
Indep Armd Sqns	2	(plus 2 tps PT-76)
Fd Regt Arty	6	
Indep Mor Bty Arty	5	
LAA Regt Arty	1	
LAA Bty Arty	1	
Frontier Corps Wings and Rangers	7	
Mujahid Bns	5	

APPENDIX 8

Deployment: East Pakistan Civil Armed Forces

EPCAF (Maj Gen Mohd Jamshed Khan, Director General)	Dacca

DACCA SECTOR

HQ	Dacca
13 Wing	Dacca area
16 Wing	Dacca

JESSORE SECTOR

HQ	Jessore
4 Wing	Chuadanga area
5 Wing	Khulna–Bagerhat–Barisal area
15 Wing	Jessore–Chaugacha area

RAJSHAHI SECTOR

HQ	Rajshahi
6 Wing	Rajshahi–Nawabganj–Rahanpur area
7 Wing	Naogaon–Patnitola area
? Wing	Bogra–Sirajganj area

RANGPUR SECTOR

HQ	Rangpur
8 Wing	Dinajpur
9 Wing	Thakurgaon–Pachagarh area
10 Wing	Rangpur–Lalmanirhat area

COMILLA SECTOR

HQ	Comilla
1 Wing	Comilla
3 Wing	Brahman Baria
12 Wing	Comilla

CHITTAGONG SECTOR

HQ	Chittagong
2 Wing	Feni area
11 Wing	Chittagong area } Elements
14 Wing	Chittagong area } in Cox's Bazar

APPENDIX 9

Grouping of Forces in Eastern Command for Operations in East Pakistan, 1971

Formation	Groupings of			
	Infantry	Armour	Artillery	Engineers
(a)	(b)	(c)	(d)	(e)
II CORPS (Lt Gen T N Raina) Corps Tps			HQ 8 Mtn Arty Bde Bty 48 AD Regt Tp 107 AD Regt (TA) 4 Air Op Flt less two Secs 11 Air Op Flt	CE Corps HQ 58 Engr Regt 268 Army Engr Regt One PI ex 702 Engr Plant Coy Det 235 IWT Op Coy with 4xRPLs and 2x40 man boats Adv Engr Pk Kankinara One PI 972 Tpt Coy ASC (Tipper) 63 Engr Regt

(a)	(b)	(c)	(d)	(e)
4 Mtn Div (Maj Gen M S Barar)	HQ 7 Mtn Bde (Brig Zail Singh) 22 Rajput, 5 Jat, Naga Regt; HQ 41 Mtn Bde (Brig Tony Michigan) 5 Guards, 9 Dogra, 5/1 GR; HQ 62 Mtn Bde (Brig Rajinder Nath) 5 Maratha LI, 4 Sikh LI, 2/9 GR	A Sqn 45 Cav	Hq 4 Mtn Arty Bde, 22 Mtn Regt (76 mm), 194 Mtn Regt (76 mm), 7 Fd Regt (25 Pr), 181 Lt Regt (120 Tempella), Bty 78 Med Regt (130 mm)	
9 Inf Div (Maj Gen Dalbir Singh)	HQ 32 Inf Bde (Brig M Tewari) 7 Punjab, 8 Madras, 13 Dorga	45 Cav less a Sqn, Sqn 63 CAV	HQ 9 Arty Bde, 6 Fd Regt (25 Pr), 14 Fd Regt (25 Pr), 67 Fd Regt (25 Pr), 78 Med Regt (130 mm) less one Bty, 88 Lt Regt (120 mm Brandt)	102 Engr Regt

(a)	(b)	(c)	(d)	(e)
			201 Div Loc Bty	
			264 SBRL Increment (Grad-P)	
	HQ 42 Inf Bde			
	(Brig Rajinder Nath)			
	14 Punjab			
	19 Maratha LI			
	2 Sikh LI			
	HQ 350 Inf Bde			
	(Brig H S Sandhu)			
	26 Madras			
	4 Sikh			
	1 J&K Rif			
MAIN IV CORPS				
(Lt Gen Sagat Singh)				
Corps Tps		No 1 Indep Sqn 7 Cav	HQ IV Corps Arty Bde	CE IV Corps
		No 5 Indep Sqn 63 Cav	Tp 46 Ad Regt (L/60)	4 Engr Regt
		No 5 Ad-hoc Sqn Ferret Cars	124 Div Loc Bty	62 Engr Regt
			24 Med Regt	234 Army Engr Regt
			Bty 48 Ad Regt	967 Engr Wksp and Pk Coy
			6 Air Op Flt	Engr Park/Advance Parks
			11 Air Op Flt	Parks Silchar/Dharamnagar/
				Teliamura

(a)	(b)	(c)	(d)	(e)
8 Mtn Div (Maj Gen K V Krishna Rao)	HQ 59 Mtn Bde (Brig C A Quinn) 9 Guards 6 Rajput 4/5 GR		HQ 2 Mtn Arty Bde 99 Mtn Regt (75/24 mm) 93 Mtn Regt (75/24 mm) Bty 85 Lt Regt (120 Brandt) Bty 40 Med Regt (5.5 in)	971 Tpt Coy ASC (Tipper) 108 Engr Regt
	HQ 81 Mtn Bde (Brig R C V Apte) 3 Punjab 4 Kumaon 10 Mahar			
23 Mtn Div (Maj Gen R D Hira)	HQ 83 Mtn Bde (Brig B S Sandhu) 2 Rajput 3 Dogra 8 Bihar		HQ 23 Mtn Arty Bde 57 Mtn Regt (76 mm) 197 Mtn Regt (76 mm) 198 Mtn Regt (76 mm) 183 Lt Regt (120 Brandt)	3 Engr Regt
	HQ 181 Mtn Bde (Brig Y C Bakshi) 6 Jat 9 Kumaon 18 Kumaon		262 SBRL Increment (Grad-P)	

194

(a)	(b)	(c)	(d)	(e)
	HQ 301 Mtn Bde (Brig H S Sodhi) 14 Jat 3 Kumaon 1/11 GR			15 Engr Regt
57 Mtn Div (Maj Gen B F Gonsalves)	HQ 61 Mtn Bde (Brig Tom Pande) 7 Raj Rif 2 Jat 12 Kumaon		HQ 57 Mtn Arty Bde 23 Mtn Regt (75/24 mm) 59 Mtn Regt (75/24 mm) 65 Mtn Regt (75/24 mm) 82 Lt Regt (120 Brandt) 124 Div Loc Bty	
	HQ 73 Mtn Bde (Brig Tuli) 14 Guards 19 Punjab 19 Raj Rif			
	HQ 311 Mtn Bde (Brig Misra) 4 Guards 18 Rajput 10 Bihar			

(a)	(b)	(c)	(d)	(e)
Mizo Hills Range	(Allotted to Kilo Force) HQ Mizo Hills Range 31 Jat (Mod I) 32 Mahar (Mod I)			
Ex 2 Mtn Div	HQ 5 Mtn Bde 3 Rajput 2 Dogra 2 Garh Rif	Allotted to 101 Comn Z for Dacca thrust		
Ex 5 Mtn Div	Hq 167 Mtn Bde 6 Sikh LI 6 Bihar 10 J & K Rif	Allotted to 101 Comn Z for Dacca thrust	Allotted by Eastern Command in November. Released by Army HQ for employment on 8 Dec.	
XXXIII CORPS (Lt Gen M L Thapan) Corps Tps		63 Cav less Sqn 69 Armd Regt	HQ XXXIII Corps Arty Bde Bty 46 AD Regt Two Secs 4 Air Op Flt 15 Air Op Flt	CE XXXIII Corps HQ 471 Engr Bde 11 Engr Regt 52 Engr Regt 111 Engr Regt 235 Army Engr Regt 651 Engr Plant Coy 342 Engr Wksp and Pk Coy

196

(a)	(b)	(c)	(d)	(e)
				585 Engr Park Bengdubi Br Coy Normal 1133 ASC Bn 972 Tpt Coy ASC (Tipper) less one Pl
6 Mtn Div (Maj Gen P C Reddy)	HQ 9 Mtn Bde 5 Grenadiers 4 Rajput		HQ 6 Mtn Arty Bde 94 Mtn Regt (75 mm USA) 98 Mtn Regt (75 mm USA) 184 Lt Regt less one Bty (120 Brandt)	51 Engr Regt
	HQ 99 Mtn Bde 18 Sikh 11 Garh Rif 16 Kumaon	Army HQ reserve for Bhutan		
20 Mtn Div (Maj Gen Lachhman Singh)	HQ 66 Mtn Bde (Brig G S Sharma) 1 Guards 6 Guards 17 Kumaon		HQ 20 Mtn Arty Bde 64 Mtn Regt (75/28 mm) 95 Mtn Regt (75/24 mm) 100 Mtn Regt (75/24 mm) 33 Lt Regt (120 Brandt) 38 Med Regt (5.5 in)	13 Engr Regt
	HQ 165 Mtn Bde (Brig R S Pannu) 20 Maratha LI 16 Rajput 6 Assam			

(a)	(b)	(c)	(d)	(e)
	HQ 202 Mtn Bde (Brig F P Bhatty) 8 Guards 22 Maratha LI 5 Garh Rif			
	HQ 164 Mtn Bde 9 Grenadiers 1 Assam 2/1 GR			
340 Mtn Bde Gp	HQ 340 Mtn Bde Gp (Brig Joginder Singh) 4 Madras 2/5 GR 5/11 GR		97 Mtn Regt (75/24 mm)	
71 Mtn Bde (under Corps HQ)	HQ 71 Mtn Bde (P N Kathpalia) 7 Maratha LI 12 Raj Rif 21 Rajput			

(a)	(b)	(c)	(d)	(e)
50 Indep Para Bde (Brig M Thomas)	HQ 50 Indep Para Bde 2 Para 7 Para 8 Para		17 Para Fd Regt (75 mm USA)	411 Para Fd Coy
Bengal Area	1/3 GR 11 Bihar 12 Garh Rif			CE Bengal Zone 261 Bomb Disposal Pl 8 Engr E and M Coy
101 Comn Z area (Maj Gen Gurbax Singh, Maj Gen G C Nagra)	HQ 95 Mtn Bde (Brig H S Kler) 13 Guards 1 Maratha LI 13 Raj Rif 5/5 GR	Allotted 167 and 5 Mtn Bdes	56 Mtn Regt (76 mm) Bty 85 Lt Regt (120 Brandt) Bty 90 Mtn Regt (75/24 mm) Bty 85 Lt Regt (120 Brandt)	CE/North Eastern Zone 94 Fd Coy ex 59 Engr Regt 262 Bomb Disposal Pl 583 Engr Pk Narangi 584 Engr Pk Jorhat
312 Indep AD Bde	Moved to Western Sector 6 Dec		HQ 312 Indep AD Bde 19 AD Regt (L70) 28 AD Regt (L/60) 46 AD Regt less three tps (L/60) Bty 48 AD Regt (L/60)	

(a)	(b)	(c)	(d)	(e)
342 Indep AD Bde	Moved to Western Sector 6 Dec		HQ 342 Indep AD Bde 25 AD Regt (L/70) 47 AD Regt (L/60) 48 AD Regt less one By (L/60)	
Comd reserve				203 Army Engr Regt 457 IWT Engrs and one Pl 235 IWT Op Coy ESD Panagar HQ 191 Bomb Disposal Gp

APPENDIX 10

Own Casualties

Formations	Officers			JCOs			OR			NCOs		
	Killed	Wounded	Missing	Killed	Wounded	Missing	Killed	Wounded	Missing	Killed	Wounded	Missing
II Corps	17	55	-	20	50	-	330	1174	5	1	3	-
IV Corps	25	84	-	23	58	-	488	1400	23	2	5	-
XXXIII Corps	16	54	-	11	33	2	344	874	8	-	2	-
Bengal Area	-	-	-	-	-	-	2	3	-	-	-	-
101 Comn Zone Area	7	17	-	6	19	1	123	225	17	-	1	-
50 Indep Para Bde	3	1	-	-	-	-	3	-	-	-	-	-
TOTAL	68	211	-	60	160	3	1290	3676	53	3	11	-

APPENDIX 11

The Awami League's Six Points
Extract from Awami League Manifesto

Pakistan shall be a Federation granting full autonomy on the basis of the six-point formula to each of the federating units:

Point No. 1

The character of the government shall be federal and parliamentary, in which the election to the federal legislature and to the legislatures of the federating units shall be direct and on the basis of universal adult franchise. The representation in the federal legislature shall be on the basis of population.

Point No. 2

The federal government shall be responsible only for defence and foreign affairs and subject to the conditions provided in (3) below, currency.

Point No. 3

There shall be two separate currencies mutually or freely convertible in each wing for each region, or in the alternative a single currency, subject to the establishment of federal reserve system in which there will be regional federal reserve banks which shall devise measures to prevent the transfer of resources and flight of capital from one region to another.

Point No. 4

Fiscal policy shall be the responsibility of the federating units. The federal government shall be provided with requisite revenue resources for meeting the requirements of defence and foreign affairs, which revenue resources would be automatically appropriable by the federal government in the manner provided and on the basis of the ratio to be determined by the procedure laid down in the constitution. Such constitutional provisions would ensure that federal government's revenue requirements are met consistently with the objective of ensuring control over the fiscal

202

policy by the governments of the federating units.

Point No. 5

Constitutional provisions shall be made to enable separate accounts to be maintained of the foreign exchange earnings of each of the federating units, under the control of the respective governments of the federating units. The foreign exchange requirement of the federal government shall be met by the governments of the federating units on the basis of a ratio to be determined in accordance with the procedure laid down in the constitution. The regional governments shall have power under the constitution to negotiate foreign trade and aid within the framework of the foreign policy of the country, which shall be the responsibility of the federal government.

Point No. 6.

The government of the federating units shall be empowered to maintain a militia or para-military force in order to contribute effectively towards national security.

Source: *The Government of Pakistan White Paper.*

President Yahya Khan's Broadcast of
26 March 1971

My dear countrymen,

Assalam-o-Alaikum,

On the 6 of this month I announced 25 March as the new date for the inaugural session of the National Assembly hoping that conditions would permit the holding of the session on the appointed date. Events have, however, not justified that hope. The nation continued to face a grave crisis.

In East Pakistan a non-co-operation and disobedience movement was launched by the Awami League and matters took a very serious turn. Events were moving very fast and it became absolutely imperative that the situation was brought under control as soon as possible. With this aim in view, I had a series of discussions with political leaders in West Pakistan and subsequently on 15 March I went to Dacca.

As you are aware I had a number of meetings with Sheikh Mujibur Rehman in order to resolve the political impasse. Having consulted West Pakistan leaders it was necessary for me to do the same over there so that areas of agreement could be identified and an amicable settlement arrived at.

As has been reported in the Press and other news media from time to time, my talks with Sheikh Mujibur Rehman showed some progress. Having reached a certain stage in my negotiations with Sheikh Mujibur Rehman I considered it necessary to have another round of talks with West Pakistani leaders in Dacca.

Mr Z. A. Bhutto reached there on 21 March and I had a number of meetings with him.

As you are aware, the leader of the Awami League had asked for the withdrawal of Martial Law and transfer of power prior to the meeting of the National Assembly. In our discussions he proposed that this interim period could be covered by a proclamation by me whereby Martial Law would be withdrawn, provincial Governments set up and the National Assembly would, *ab initio*, sit in two committees—one composed of members from East Pakistan and the other composed of members from West Pakistan.

Despite some serious flaws in the scheme, in its legal as well as other aspects, I was prepared to agree in principle to this plan in the interest of peaceful transfer of power but on one condition. The condition which I clearly explained to Sheikh Mujibur Rehman was that I must first have unequivocal agreement of all political leaders to the scheme.

I thereupon discussed the proposal with other political leaders. I found them unanimously of the view that the proposed proclamation by me would have no legal sanction. It will neither have the cover of Martial Law nor could it claim to be based on the will of the people. Thus a vacuum would be created and chaotic conditions will ensue. They also considered that splitting of the National Assembly into two parts through a proclamation would encourage divisive tendencies that may exist. They, therefore expressed the opinion that if it is intended to lift Martial Law and transfer power in the interim period, the National Assembly should meet, pass an appropriate interim Constitution Bill and present it for my assent. I entirely agreed with their view and requested them to tell Sheikh Mujibur Rehman to take a reasonable attitude on this issue.

I told the leaders to explain their views to him that a scheme whereby, on the one hand, you extinguish all source of power, namely, Martial Law and, on the other, fail to replace it by the will of the people through a proper session of the National Assembly, will merely result in chaos. They agreed to meet Sheikh Mujibur Rehman, explain the position and try to obtain his agreement to the interim arrangement for transfer of power to emanate from the National Assembly.

The political leaders were also very much perturbed over Sheikh Mujib's idea of dividing the National Assembly into two parts right from start. Such a move, they felt, would be totally against the interest of Pakistan's integrity.

The Chairman of the Pakistan People's Party, during the meeting

205

between myself, Sheikh Mujibur Rehman and him had also expressed similar views to Mujib.

On the evening of 23 March the political leaders, who had gone to talk to Mujib on this issue, called on me and informed me that he was not agreeable to any changes in his scheme. All he really wanted was for me to make a proclamation, whereby I should withdraw Martial Law and transfer power.

Sheikh Mujibur Rehman's action of starting his non-co-operation movement is an act of treason. He and his Party have defied the lawful authority for over three weeks. They have insulted Pakistan's flag and defiled the photograph of the Father of the Nation. They have tried to run a parallel government. They have created turmoil, terror and insecurity.

A number of murders have been committed in the name of the movement. Millions of our Bengali brethren and those who have settled in East Pakistan are living in a state of panic, and a very large number had to leave that Wing out of fear for their lives.

The Armed Forces, located in East Pakistan, have been subjected to taunts and insults of all kinds. I wish to compliment them on the tremendous restraint that they have shown in the face of grave provocation. Their sense of discipline is indeed praiseworthy. I am proud of them.

I should have taken action against Sheikh Mujibur Rehman and his collaborators weeks ago but I had to try my utmost to handle the situation in such a manner as not to jeopardize my plan of peaceful transfer of power. In my keenness to achieve this aim I kept to tolerating one illegal act after another, and at the same time I explored every possible avenue for arriving at some reasonable solution. I have already mentioned the efforts made by me and by various political leaders in getting Sheikh Mujibur Rehman to see reason. We have left no stone unturned. But he has failed to respond in any constructive manner; on the other hand, he and his followers kept on flouting the authority of the Government even during my presence in Dacca. The proclamation that he proposed was nothing but a trap. He knew that it would not have been worth the paper it was written on and in the vacuum created by the lifting of Martial Law he could have done anything with impunity. His obstinacy, obduracy and absolute refusal to talk sense can lead to

206

but one conclusion—the man and his Party are enemies of Pakistan and they want East Pakistan to break away completely from the country. He has attacked the solidarity and integrity of this country—his crime will not go unpunished.

We will not allow some power-hungry and unpatriotic people to destroy this country and play with the destiny of 120 million people.

In my address to the Nation of 6 March I told you that it is the duty of the Pakistan Armed Forces to ensure the integrity, solidarity and security of Pakistan. I have ordered them to do their duty and fully restore the authority of the Government.

In view of the grave situation that exists in the country today I have decided to ban all political activities throughout the country. As for the Awami League, it is completely banned as a political party. I have also decided to impose complete press censorship. Martial Law Regulations will very shortly be issued in pursuance of these decisions.

In the end let me assure you that my main aim remains the same, namely, transfer of power to the elected representatives of the people. As soon as situation permits I will take fresh steps towards the achievement of this objective.

It is my hope that the law and order situation will soon return to normal in East Pakistan and we can again move forward towards our cherished goal.

I appeal to my countrymen to appreciate the gravity of the situation, for which blame rests entirely on the anti-Pakistan and secessionist elements, and to act as reasonable citizens of the country because therein lies the security and salvation of Pakistan.

God be with you. God bless you.

PAKISTAN PAINDABAD

Source: *Pakistan Horizon*, XXIV, No. 2, pp. 107-10.

Resolution of the Indian Parliament 31 March 1971
Moved by Mrs Indira Gandhi

This House expresses its deep anguish and grave concern at the recent developments in East Bengal. A massive attack by armed forces, despatched from West Pakistan, has been unleashed against the entire people of East Bengal with a view to suppressing their urges and aspirations.

Instead of respecting the will of the people so unmistakably expressed through the election in Pakistan in December 1970, the Government of Pakistan has chosen to flout the mandate of the people.

The Government of Pakistan has not only refused to transfer power to legally elected representatives but has arbitrarily prevented the National Assembly from assuming its rightful and sovereign role. The people of East Bengal are being sought to be suppressed by the naked use of force, by bayonets, machine guns, tanks, artillery and aircraft.

The Government and people of India have always desired and worked for peaceful, normal and fraternal relations with Pakistan. However, situated as India is and bound as the people of the sub-continent are by centuries-old ties of history, culture and tradition, this House cannot remain indifferent to the macabre tragedy being enacted so close to our border. Throughout the length and breadth of our land, our people have condemned, in unmistakable terms, the atrocities now being perpetrated on an unprecedented scale upon an unarmed and innocent people.

This House expresses its profound sympathy for and solidarity with the people of East Bengal in their struggle for a democratic way of life.

Bearing in mind the permanent interests which India has in peace, and committed as we are to uphold and defend human rights, this House demands immediate cessation of the use of force and the massacre of defenceless people. This House calls upon all peoples and Governments of the world to take urgent and constructive steps to prevail upon the Government of Pakistan to put an end immediately to the systematic decimation of people which amounts to genocide.

This House records its profound conviction that the historic upsurge of the 75 million people of East Bengal will triumph. The House wishes to assure them that their struggle and sacrifices will receive the wholehearted sympathy and support of the people of India.

Source: *Bangla Desh Documents,* p. 672.

APPENDIX 14

President Nikolai Podgorny's Letter to President Yahya Khan of 2 April 1971

Esteemed Mr President,

The report that the talks in Dacca had been broken off and that the Military Administration had found it possible to resort to extreme measures and used armed force against the population of East Pakistan was met with great alarm in the Soviet Union.

Soviet people cannot but be concerned by the numerous casualties, by the sufferings and privations that such a development of events brings to the people of Pakistan. Concern is also caused in the Soviet Union by the arrest and persecution of M. Rehman and other politicians who had received such convincing support by the overwhelming majority of the people of East Pakistan at the recent general elections. Soviet people have always sincerely wished the people of Pakistan all the best and prosperity and rejoiced at their success in solving in a democratic manner the complex problems that face the country.

In these days of trial for the Pakistani people we cannot but say a few words coming from true friends. We have been and remain convinced that the complex problems that have arisen in Pakistan of late can and must be solved politically without use of force. Continuation of repressive measures and blood-shed in East Pakistan will undoubtedly only make the solution of the problems more difficult and may do great harm to the vital interest of the entire people of Pakistan.

We consider it our duty to address you, Mr President, on behalf of the Presidium of the Supreme Soviet of the USSR, with an insistent appeal for the adoption of the most urgent measures to stop the blood-shed and repression against the population in East Pakistan and for turning to methods of a peaceful political settlement. We are convinced that this would meet the interest of the entire people of Pakistan and the interest of preserving peace in the area. A peaceful solution of the problems that have arisen would be received with satisfaction by the entire Soviet people.

In appealing to you we were guided by the generally recognized humanitarian principles recorded in the universal Declaration of Human Rights and by [concern for] the welfare of the friendly people of Pakistan.

We hope, Mr President, that you will correctly interpret the motives by which we are guided in making this appeal. It is our sincere wish that tranquility and justice be established in East Pakistan in the shortest possible time.

Source: *Bangla Desh Documents*, pp. 510-11.

APPENDIX 15

Mr Chou En-lai's Letter to
President Yahya Khan of 13 April 1971

I have read Your Excellency's letter and Ambassador Chang Tung's report on Your Excellency's conversation with him. I am grateful to Your Excellency for your trust in the Chinese Government. China and Pakistan are friendly neighbours. The Chinese Government and people are following with close concern the development of the present situation in Pakistan. Your Excellency and leaders of various quarters in Pakistan have done a lot of useful work to uphold the unification of Pakistan and to prevent it from moving towards a split. We believe that through the wise consultations and efforts of Your Excellency and leaders of various quarters in Pakistan, the situation in Pakistan will certainly be restored to normal. In our opinion, the unification of Pakistan and the unity of the people of East and West Pakistan are the basic guarantees for Pakistan to attain prosperity and strength. Here, it is most important to differentiate the broad masses of the people from a handful of persons who want to sabotage the unification of Pakistan. As a genuine friend of Pakistan, we would like to present these views for Your Excellency's reference.

At the same time, we have noted that of late the Indian Government has been carrying out gross interference in the internal affairs of Pakistan by exploiting the internal problems of your country. And the Soviet Union and the United States are doing the same one after the other. The Chinese Press is carrying reports to expose such unreasonable interference and has published Your Excellency's letter of reply to Podgorny. The Chinese Government holds that what is happening in Pakistan at present is purely the internal affair of Pakistan, which can only be settled by the Pakistan people themselves and which brooks no foreign interference whatsoever. Your Excellency may rest assured that should the Indian expansionists dare to launch aggression against Pakistan, the Chinese Government and people will, as always, firmly support the Pakistan Government and people in their just struggle to safeguard State sovereignty and national independence.

Source: *Pakistan Horizon*, XXIV, No. 2, pp. 153-4.

U Thant's Memorandum to the President of the Security Council, 19 July 1971

For some months now members of the Security Council and many other members of the United Nations have been deeply preoccupied with developments in East Pakistan and adjacent Indian States and their consequences or possible consequences. I, myself, expressed my concern over the situation to President Yahya Khan shortly after the events of March 1971 and have been in continuous touch with the Governments of Pakistan and India, both through their Permanent Representatives at the United Nations and through other contacts. In these exchanges I have been acutely aware of the dual responsibility of the United Nations, including the Secretary-General under the Charter, both to observe the provisions of article 2, paragraph 7 and to work within the framework of international economic and social cooperation to help promote and ensure human well-being and humanitarian principles.

It was with this latter responsibility in mind that I appealed for assistance both for refugees from East Pakistan now in India and for the population of East Pakistan. In order to channel assistance given in response to those appeals, I designated the United Nations High Commissioner for Refugees as focal point for assistance to refugees in India and appointed with the agreement of the Government of Pakistan, a Representative in Dacca in order to make as effective use as possible of international assistance made available for relief of the population of East Pakistan. Both of these humanitarian efforts have been reported upon in detail elsewhere and the Economic and Social Council held a full discussion on both operations on 16 July 1971. Based on statements to the Council by the United Nations High Commissioner for Refugees and the Assistant Secretary-General for Inter-Agency Affairs, I take this opportunity to express my warm gratitude to the Governments,

United Nations Agencies and programmes and to the voluntary organizations which have responded generously to my appeals. I also wish to express my appreciation to the Governments of India and Pakistan for their co-ordination with my representatives in the field.

As weeks have passed since last March, I have become increasingly uneasy and apprehensive at the steady deterioration of the situation in the region in almost all its aspects. In spite of the generous response of the international community to my appeals for assistance for refugees from East Pakistan now in India, the money and supplies made available are still nowhere near sufficient and the Indian Government still faces the appalling and disruptive problem of caring for an unforeseeable period of time for millions of refugees whose number is still increasing. In East Pakistan international and governmental efforts to cope with results of two successive disasters, one of them natural, are increasingly hampered by the lack of substantial progress towards a political reconciliation and the consequent effect on law, order and public administration in East Pakistan. There is a danger that serious food shortages and even famine could soon add to the suffering of the population unless conditions can be improved to the point where a large scale relief programme can be effecitve. Equally serious is the undoubted fact that reconciliation, an improved political atmosphere and success of relief efforts are indispensable prerequisites for the return of any large proportion of the refugees now in India. The situation is one in which political, economic and social factors have produced a series of vicious circles which largely frustrate efforts of the authorities concerned and of international community to deal with the vast humanitarian problems involved.

These human tragedies have consequences in a far wider sphere. Violent emotions aroused could have repercussions on the relations of religious and ethnic groups in the subcontinent as a whole and relationship of the Government of India and Pakistan is also a major component of the problem. Conflict between principles of the territorial integrity of States and of self-determination has often before in history given rise to fratricidal strife and has provoked in recent years highly emotional reactions

215

in the international community. In the present case there is an additional element of danger, for the crisis is unfolding in the context of long standing and unresolved differences between India and Pakistan, differences which gave rise to open warfare only six years ago. Although there can be no question of deep desire of both Governments for peace, tension between them shows no sign of subsiding. The situation on the borders of East Pakistan is particularly disturbing. Border clashes, clandestine raids and acts of sabotage appear to be becoming more frequent and this is all the more serious since refugees must cross this disturbed border, if repatriation is to become a reality. Nor can any of us here in the United Nations afford to forget that a major conflict in the subcontinent could all too easily expand.

In the tragic circumstances such as those prevailing in the sub-continent, it is all too easy to make moral judgements. It is far more difficult to face up to political and human realities of the situation and to help the peoples concerned to find a way out of their enormous difficulties. It is this latter course which in my view the United Nations must follow.

I do not think I have painted too dark a picture of the present situation and of its possible consequences. In the light of information available to me I have reluctantly come to the conclusion that the time is past when the international community can continue to stand by watching the situation deteriorate and hoping that relief programmes, humanitarian efforts and good intentions will be enough to turn the tide of human misery and potential disaster. I am deeply concerned about the possible consequences of the present situation not only in the humanitarian sense but also as a potential threat to peace and security and for its bearing on the future of the United Nations as an efffective instrument for international co-operation and action. It seems to me that the present tragic situation, in which humanitarian, economic and political problems are mixed in such a way as almost to defy any distinction between them, presents a challenge to the United Nations as a whole which must be met. Other situations of this kind may well occur in the future. If the Organization faces up to such a situation now it may be able to develop new skill and new strength required to face future situations of this kind.

It is for these reasons that I am taking the unusual step of reporting to the President of the Council on a question which has not been inscribed on the Council's agenda. The political aspects of this matter are of such far-reaching importance that the Secretary-General is not in a position to suggest precise courses of action before members of the Security Council have taken note of the problem. I believe, however, that the United Nations with its long experience in peace-keeping and with its varied resources for conciliation and persuasion, must and should now play a more forthright role in attempting both to mitigate human tragedy which has already taken place and to avert further deterioration of the situation.

The Security Council, the world's highest body for the maintenance of international peace and security, is in a position to consider with the utmost attention and concern, the present situation and to reach some agreed conclusions as to the measures which might be taken. Naturally it is for members of the Council themselves to decide whether such consideration should take place formally or informally, in public or in private. My primary purpose at this stage is to provide a basis and an opportunity for such discussions to take place and to express my grave concern that all possible ways and means should be explored which might help to resolve this tragic situation.

The suggestion is simply that a small number of representatives of the High Commissioner might take to field with strictly limited terms of reference and on an experimental basis. The area in which these representatives might operate would be decided upon by the Governments concerned in consultations with the United Nations High Commissioner for Refugees. This suggestion was made with the sole aim of facilitating, if possible, repatriation of refugees.

The other document (the memorandum by U Thant to the President of the Security Council) deals with a far-reaching political matter relating to international peace and security and is primarily within the competence of the Security Council, apart from the Secretary-General's competence under the Charter in such matters. I recall that at its 1329th meeting on 2 December 1966, members of the Security Council unanimously endorsed a statement that 'they fully respect his—the Secretary-General's—position and his action in bringing basic issues confronting the Organisation and disturbing developments in many parts of the world to their notice'.

The memorandum is not an official document of the Security Council and was intended to record my own deep concern with the wider potential dangers of the situation in the region and to provide an opportunity for an exchange of views among members of the Security Council on the potentially very grave situation.

Source: *Pakistan Horizon*, XXIV, No. 3, pp. 127-30.

The Indo-Soviet Treaty of Peace, Friendship and Co-operation, 9 August 1971

Desirous of expanding and consolidating the existing relations of sincere friendship between them,

Believing that the further development of friendship and co-operation meets the basic national interests of lasting peace in Asia and the world,

Determined to promote the consolidation of universal peace and security and to make steadfast efforts for the relaxation of international tensions and the final eliminations of the remnants of colonialism,

Upholding their firm faith in the principles of peaceful co-existence and co-operation between States with different political and social systems,

Convinced that in the world today international problems can only be solved by co-operation and not by conflict,

Reaffirming their determination to abide by the purposes and principles of the United Nations Charter,

The Republic of India on the one side, and the Union of Soviet Socialist Republics on the other side,

Have decided to conclude the present treaty, for which purposes the following plenipotentiaries have been appointed:

On behalf of the Republic of India: Sardar Swaran Singh. Minister of External Affairs.

On behalf of the Union of Soviet Socialist Republics: Mr A. A. Gromyko, Minister of Foreign Affairs.

Who, having each presented their credentials, which are found to be in proper form and due order, have agreed as follows:

(ARTICLE I)

The High Contracting Parties solemnly declare that enduring peace and friendship shall prevail between the two countries and their peoples. Each party shall respect the independence, sovereignty and territorial integrity of the other party and refrain from interfering in the other's internal affairs. The High Contracting Parties shall continue to develop and consolidate the relations of sincere friendship, good neighbourliness and comprehensive co-operation existing between them on the basis of the aforesaid principles as well as those of equality and mutual benefit.

(ARTICLE II)

Guided by the desire to contribute in every possible way to ensure enduring peace and security of their people, the High Contracting Parties declare their determination to continue their efforts to preserve and to strengthen peace in Asia and throughout the world, to halt the arms race and to achieve general and complete disarmament, including both nuclear and conventional, under effective international control.

(ARTICLE III)

Guided by their loyalty to the lofty ideal of equality of all peoples and nations, irrespective of race or creed, the High Contracting Parties condemn colonialism and racialism in all forms and manifestations, and reaffirm their determination to strive for their final and complete elimination.

The High Contracting Parties shall cooperate with other States to achieve these aims and to support the just aspirations of the peoples in their struggle against colonialism and racial domination.

(ARTICLE IV)

The Republic of India respects the peace-loving policy of the Union of Soviet Socialist Republics aimed at strengthening friendship and co-operation with all nations.

The Union of Soviet Socialist Republics respects India's policy of non-alignment and reaffirms that this policy constitutes an important factor in the maintenance of universal peace and international security and in the lessening of tensions in the world.

(ARTICLE V)

Deeply interested in ensuring universal peace and security, attaching great importance to their mutual co-operation in the international field for achieving these aims, the High Contracting

Parties will maintain regular contacts with each other on major international problems affecting the interests of both the States by means of meetings, and exchanges of views between their leading statesmen, visits by official delegations and special envoys of the two Governments, and through diplomatic channels.

(ARTICLE VI)

Attaching great importance to economic, scientific and technological co-operation between them, the High Contracting Parties will continue to consolidate and expand mutually advantageous and comprehensive co-operation in these fields as well as expand trade, transport and communications between them on the basis of the principles of equality, mutual benefit and most-favoured nation treatment, subject to the existing agreements and the special arrangements with contiguous countries as specified in the Indo-Soviet trade agreement of 26 December 1970.

(ARTICLE VII)

The High Contracting Parties shall promote further development of ties and contacts between them in the fields of science, art, literature, education, public health, press, radio, television, cinema, tourism and sports.

(ARTICLE VIII)

In accordance with the traditional friendship established between the two countries, each of the High Contracting Parties solemnly declares that it shall not enter into or participate in any military alliance directed against the other Party.

Each High Contracting Party undertakes to abstain from any aggression against the other Party and to prevent the use of its territory for the commission of any act which might inflict military damage on the other High Contracting Party.

(ARTICLE IX)

Each High Contracting Party undertakes to abstain from providing any assistance to any third country that engages in armed conflict with the other Party. In the event of either being subjected to an attack or a threat thereof, the High Contracting Parties shall immediately enter into mutual consultations in order to remove such threat and to take appropriate effective measures to ensure peace and the security of their countries.

(ARTICLE X)

Each High Contracting Party solemnly declares that it shall not enter into any obligation, secret or public, with one or more States, which is incompatible with this Treaty. Each High Contracting Party further declares that no obligation be entered into, between itself and any other State or States, which might cause military damage to the other Party.

(ARTICLE XI)

This Treaty is concluded for the duration of twenty years and will be automatically extended for each successive period of five years unless either High Contracting Party declares its desire to terminate it by giving notice to the other High Contracting Party twelve months prior to the expiration of the Treaty. The Treaty will be subject to ratification and will come into force on the date of the exchange of Instruments of Ratification which will take place in Moscow within one month of the signing of this Treaty.

(ARTICLE XII)

Any difference of interpretation of any Article or Articles of this Treaty which may arise between the High Contracting Parties will be settled bilaterally by peaceful means in a spirit of mutual respect and understanding.

The said Plenipotentiaries have signed the present Treaty in Hindi, Russian and English, all text being equally authentic and have affixed thereto their seals.

Done in New Delhi on the Ninth day of August in the year One Thousand Nine Hundred and Seventy One.

On behalf of the Union of Soviet Socialist Republics
(Sd.) A. A. Gromyko,
Minister of External Affairs,
On behalf of the Republic of India
(Sd.) Swaran Singh,
Minister of External Affairs.

Source: *Survival,* XIII, October 1971, pp. 351-3.

APPENDIX 18

Mr Chi Peng-fei's Statement of 7 November 1971

A Pakistan delegation, under the leadership of Z. A. Bhutto, visited China from 5 to 8 November. China's Acting Foreign Minister, Chi Peng-fei, gave a banquet in honour of the visiting Pakistani delegation on 7 November 1971. In his welcome speech, Mr Chi Peng-fei said: 'The friendly relations and co-operation between our two countries and the friendship between our two peoples have been consolidated and developed continuously.'

He spoke highly of the Pakistan people who had a glorious tradition of opposing imperialism and expansionism. He said: 'In order to defend their state sovereignty, territorial integrity and national independence, they have waged unremitting struggles against foreign aggressors, interventionists and domestic secessionists. The Pakistan Government has adhered to its foreign policy of independence and contributed to the defence of peace in Asia and the promotion of Afro-Asian solidarity.'

Chi Peng-fei continued: 'Of late, the Indian Government has crudely interfered in Pakistan's internal affairs, carried out subversive activities and military threats against Pakistan by continuing to exploit the East Pakistan question. The Chinese Government and people are greatly concerned over the present tension in the sub-continent. We maintain that the internal affairs of any country must be handled by its own people. The East Pakistan question is the internal affair of Pakistan and a reasonable settlement should be sought by the Pakistan people themselves, and it is absolutely impermissible for any foreign country to carry out interference and subversion under any pretext. Consistently abiding by the Five Principles of peaceful co-existence, the Chinese Government never interferes in the internal affairs of other countries and firmly opposes any country interfering in the internal affairs of other countries. This is our firm and unshakable stand. We believe that the broad masses of the Pakistan people are patriotic

223

and they want to safeguard national unity and unification of the country, oppose internal split and outside interference. It is our hope that the Pakistan people will strengthen their unity and make joint efforts to overcome difficulties and solve their own problems. We have noted that certain persons are truculently exerting pressure on Pakistan by exploiting tension in the sub-continent, in a wild attempt to realize their ulterior motives. The Chinese Government and people have always held that disputes between states should be settled by the two sides concerned through consultations and not by resorting to force. The reasonable proposal put forward recently by President Yahya Khan for the armed forces of India and Pakistan to withdraw from the border respectively and disengage is helpful to easing tension in the sub-continent and should be received with welcome. Our Pakistan friends may rest assured that should Pakistan be subjected to foreign aggression, the Chinese Government and people will, as always, resolutely support the Pakistan Government and people in their just struggle to defend their state sovereignty and national independence.'

Source: J. A. Naik, *India, Russia, China and Bangla Desh* (New Delhi: S. Chand, 1972).

Dr Henry Kissinger's Press Briefing of 7 December 1971 and Mr Kenneth Keating's Comments

(A) Excerpts from a background briefing for a news conference given on 7 December by Henry A. Kissinger, President Nixon's adviser on national security. Senator Barry Goldwater of Arizona obtained the transcript from the White House and inserted it in *The Congressional Record* on 9 December. It constitutes a Nixon Administration summary of American policy at the time of the meeting discussed in the documents made public on 5 January.

OPENING STATEMENT

There have been some comments that the Administration is anti-Indian. This is totally inaccurate. India is a great country. It is the most populous free country. It is governed by democratic procedures.

Americans through all administrations in the postwar period have felt a commitment to the progress and development of India, and the American people have contributed to this to the extent of $10-billion.

Therefore, when we have differed with India, as we have in recent weeks, we do so with great sadness and with great disappointment.

Now let me describe the situation as we saw it, going back to 25 March. 25 March is, of course, the day when the central Government of Pakistan decided to established military rule in East Bengal and started the process which has led to the present situation.

The United States has never supported the particular action that led to this tragic series of events, and the United States has always recognized that this action has consequences which had a considerable impact on India. We have always recognized that the influx of refugees into India produced the danger of communal strife in a country always precariously poised on the edge of communal strife. We have known that it is a strain on the already scarce economic resources of a country in the process of development.

The United States position has been to attempt two efforts simultaneously: one, to ease the human suffering and to bring about the return of the refugees; and secondly, we have attempted to bring about a political resolution of the conflict which generated the refugees in the first place.

Now the United States did not condone what happened in March 1971; on the contrary, the United States has made no new development loans to Pakistan since March 1971.

Secondly, there has been a great deal of talk about military supplies to Pakistan. The fact of the matter is that immediately after the actions in East Pakistan at the end of March of this past year, the United States suspended any new licenses. It stopped the shipment of all military supplies out of American depots or that were under American Governmental control. The only arms that continued to be shipped to Pakistan were arms on old licenses in commercial channels, and these were spare parts. There were no lethal and end-items involved.

To give you a sense of the magnitude, the United States cut off $35-million worth of arms at the end of March of this year, or early April of this year, immediately after the actions in East Bengal, and continued to ship something less than $5-million worth; whereupon, all the remainder of the pipeline was cut off.

It is true the United States did not make any public declarations on its views of the evolution, because the United States wanted to use its influence with both Delhi and Islamabad to bring about a political settlement that would enable the refugees to return.

We attempted to promote a political settlement, and if I can sum up the difference that may have existed between us and the Government of India, it was this:

We told the Government of India on many occasions—the Secretary of State saw the Indian Ambassador 18 times; I saw him seven times since the end of August on behalf of the President. We all said that political autonomy for East Bengal was the inevitable outcome of political evolution and that we favored it. The difference may have been that the Government of India wanted things so rapidly that it was no longer talking about political evolution, but about political collapse.

We told the Indian Prime Minister when she was here of the Pakistan offer to withdraw their troops unilaterally from the border. There was no response.

We told the Indian Prime Minister when she was here that we would try to arrange negotiations between the Pakistanis and members of the Awami League, specifically approved by Mujibur, who is in prison. We told the Indian Ambassador shortly before his return to India that we were prepared even to discuss with them a political timetable, a precise timetable for the establishment of political autonomy in East Bengal.

When we say that there was no need for military action, we do not say that India did not suffer. We do not say that we are unsympathetic to India's problems or that we do not value India.

This country, which in many respects has had a love affair with India, can only, with enormous pain, accept the fact that military action was taken in our view without adequate cause, and if we express this opinion in the United Nations, we do not do so because we want to support one particular point of view on the subcontinent, or because we want to forego our friendship with what will always be one of the great countries of the world; but because we believe that if, as some of the phrases go, the right of military attack is determined by arithmetic, if political wisdom consists of saying the attacker has 500 million, and, therefore, the United States must always be on the side of numerically stronger, then we are creating a situation where, in the foreseeable future, we will have international anarchy, and where the period of peace, which is the greatest desire for the President to establish, will be jeopardized; not at first for Americans, necessarily, but for peoples all over the world.

QUESTIONS AND ANSWERS

Q. Why was the first semi-public explanation of the American position one of condemning India, and why this belated explanation that you are now giving? The perception of the world

227

is that the United States regards India as an aggressor; that it is anti-India, and you make a fairly persuasive case here that that is not the case. So why this late date?

A. We were reluctant to believe for a long time that the matter had come down to a naked recourse to force, and we were attemting for the first two weeks of the military operations to see what could be done to quiet it through personal diplomacy conducted by the Department of State.

We made two appeals to the Indian Prime Minister. We appealed also to the Pakistan President, and we appealed also to the Soviet Union.

Now, then, on Friday the situation burst into full-blown war and it was decided to put the facts before the public. Now, I cannot, of course, accept the characterization that you made of the way these facts were put forward: that they were put forward as anti-Indian.

Q. I said the perception of the world public was that the United States was anti-Indian because of the nature of that first background briefing at the State Department on Friday.

A. We are opposed to the use of military force in this crisis, and we do not believe that it was necessary to engage in military action. We believe that what started as a tragedy in East Bengal is now becoming an attempt to dismember a sovereign state and a member of the United Nations.

So the view that was expressed on Saturday is not inconsistent with the view that is expressed today. What was done today is an explanation of the background that led to the statement on Saturday, and it might have been better if we had put the whole case forward.

Source: *New York Herald Tribune*, Paris edition, 6 January 1972.

(B) A slightly paraphrased form of the text of a secret cablegram from Kenneth B. Keating, United States Ambassador to India, to William P. Rogers, the Secretary of State, on 8 December 1971, made available to *The New York Times* by the columnist Jack Anderson:

Mr Keating said he was very interested to read an article by The

International Press Service [U.S.I.A.] correspondent in the morning's wireless file reporting 'White House officials" explanation of development of present conflict and United States role in seeking to avert it. While he appreciated the tactical necessity of justfying the Administration's position publicly, he felt constrained to state that elements of this particular story do not coincide with his knowledge of the events of the past eight months.

Specifically, the I.P.S. account states that the United States Government's $155-million relief program in East Pakistan was initiated 'at the specific request of the Indian Government'. His recollection, and he referred the State Department to his conversation with Forreign Minister Swaran Singh in New Delhi on 25 May, is that the Government of India was reluctant to see the relief program started in East Pakistan prior to a political settlement on grounds that such an effort might serve to 'bail out Yahaya' [General Mohammad Agha Yahya Khan was the President of Pakistan at the time.]

In noting offer of amnesty for all refugees, story fails to mention qualification in Yahya's 5 September proclamation that amnesty applies to those 'not already charged with specific criminal acts', which Ambassador Keating took to be more than a minor bureaucratic caveat in East Pakistan circumstances.

Story indicates that both the Secretary [Mr Rogers] and Dr Kissinger informed Ambassador Jha [Lakshmi Kant Jha, Indian Ambassador to the United States] that Washington favored autonomy for East Pakistan. Mr Keating said he was aware of our repeated statements that we had no formula for a solution, and our relief that the outcome of negotiations would probably be autonomy if not independence, but he regretted that he was uninformed of any specific statement favoring autonomy.

Also according to story, Jha was informed by department on 19 November that 'Washington and Islamabad [capital of Pakistan] were prepared to discuss a precise timetable for establishing political autonomy for East Pakistan'. Ambassador Keating said the only message he had on record of this conversation [a department message to him on 21 November] makes no reference to this critical fact.

With vast and voluminous efforts of the intelligence community, reporting from both Delhi and Islamabad, and with his own discussions in Washington, Ambassador Keating said he did not understand the statement that 'Washington was not given the slightest inkling that any military operation was in any way imminent'. See [for] example DIAIB, 219-71 of 12 November [Defense Intelligence Agency Intelligence Bulletin No. 219-71, of 12 November] stating specifically that war is 'imminent'.

Statement that Pakistan had authorized U.S. to contact Mujibur through his attorney seems an overstatement, since according to Islamabad 11760 [message from American Embassy in Pakistan] Yahya on 29 November told Ambassador Farland [Joseph Farland, United States Ambassador to Pakistan] nothing more than that a Farland—Brohi meeting would be a good idea since Ambassador Farland would be able to obtain from Brohi at least his general impressions as to the state of the trial and its conduct. Mr Keating said he was unaware of any specific authorization from Yahya 'to contact Mujibur' through Brohi. [Mr Brohi was apparently the defense attorney for Sheik Mujib, leader of the East Pakistani autonomy movement, then imprisoned and on trial in West Pakistan.] In any case, as we are all only too unhappily aware, Yahya told Ambassador Farland on 2 December [Islamabad 11555] that Brohi allegedly was not interested in seeing him.

The statement on G.O.P. [Government of Pakistan] agreement on distribution by U.N. of relief supplies in East Pakistan obscures the fact that the U.N. never had nor intended to have sufficient personnel in East Pakistan to handle actual distribution, which was always in Pakistani Government hands.

Mr Keating said he made the foregoing comments in the full knowledge that they may not have been privy to all the important facts of this tragedy. On the basis of what he did know, he did not believe those elements of the story [reporting the backgrounder] either add to our position or, perhaps more importantly, to American credibility.

KEATING

Source: *New York Herald Tribune*, Paris edition, 6 January 1972.

APPENDIX 20

Minutes of the Washington Special Action Group (WSAG) Meetings of 3, 4, 6 and 8 December 1971 and Mr Jack Anderson's article of 10 January 1972*

(A) Memo on 3 December Meeting

Secret Sensitive
ASSISTANT SECRETARY OF DEFENSE
WASHINGTON, D.C. 20301

International Security Affairs Refer to: 1-29643/71

MEMORANDUM FOR RECORD

SUBJECT

WSAG meeting on India/Pakistan

PARTICIPANTS

Assistant to the President for national security affairs—Henry A. Kissinger
Under Secretary of State—John N. Irwin
Deputy Secretary of Defense—David Packard
Director, Central Intelligence Agency—Richard M. Helms
Deputy Administrator (A.I.D.)—Maurice J. Williams
Chairman, Joint Chiefs of Staff—Adm. Thomas H. Moorer
Assistant Secretary of State (N.E.E.A.R)—Joseph J. Sisco
Assistant Secretary of Defense (I.S.A.)—G. Warren Nutter
Assistant Secretary of State (I.O.)—Samuel De Palma
Principal Deputy Assistant Secretary of Defence (I.S.A.)—Armistead I. Selden Jr.
Assistant Administrator (A.I.D./N.E.S.A.)—Donald G. MacDonald

* For terms used in texts see p. 253

TIME AND PLACE

3 December 1971, 1100 hours, Situation Room, White House.

SUMMARY

Reviewed conflicting reports about major actions in the west wing. C.I.A. agreed to produce map showing areas of East Pakistan occupied by India. The President orders hold on issuance of additional irrevocable letters of credit involving $99 million, and a hold on further action implementing the $72-million P.L. 480 credit. Convening of Security Council meeting planned contingent on discussion with Pak Ambassador this afternoon plus further clarification of actual situation in West Pakistan. Kissinger asked for clarification of secret/special interpretation of March 1959, bilateral U.S. agreement with Pakistan.

KISSINGER: I am getting hell every half-hour from the President that we are not being tough on India. He has just called me again. He does not believe we are carrying out his wishes. He wants to tilt in favor of Pakistan. He feels everything we do comes out otherwise.

HELMS: Concerning the reported action in the West Wing, there are conflicting reports from both sides and the only common ground is the Pak attacks on the Amritsar, Pathankot and Srinagar airports. The Paks say the Indians are attacking all along the border; but the Indian officials say this is a lie. In the East Wing the action is becoming larger and the Paks claim there are now seven separate fronts involved.

KISSINGER: Are the Indians seizing territory?

HELMS: Yes; small bits of territory, definitely.

SISCO: It would help if you could provide a map with a shading of the areas occupied by India. What is happening in the West— is a full-scale attack likely?

MOORER: The present pattern is puzzling in that the Paks have only struck at three small airfields which do not house significant numbers of Indian combat aircraft.

HELMS: Mrs Gandhi's speech at 1:30 may well announce recognition of Bangladesh.

232

MOORER: The Pak attack is not credible. It has been made during late afternoon, which doesn't make sense. We do not seem to have sufficient facts on this yet.

KISSINGER: It is possible that the Indians attacked first and the Paks simply did what they could before dark in response?

MOORER: This is certainly possible.

KISSINGER: The President wants no more irrevocable letters of credit issued under the $99-million credit. He wants the $72-million P.L. 480 credit also held.

WILLIAMS: Word will soon get around when we do this. Does the President understand that?

KISSINGER: That is his order, but I will check with the President again. If asked, we can say we are reviewing our whole economic program and that the granting of fresh aid is being suspended in view of conditions on the subcontinent. The next issue is the U.N.

IRWIN: The Secretary is calling in the Pak Ambassador this afternoon, and the Secretary leans toward making a U.S. move in the U.N. soon.

KISSINGER: The President is in favor of this as soon as we have some confirmation of this large-scale new action. If the U.N. can't operate in this kind of situation effectively, its utility has come to an end and it is useless to think of U.N. guarantees in the Middle East.

SISCO: We will have a recommendation for you this afternoon, after the meeting with the Ambassador. In order to give the Ambassador time to wire home, we could tentatively plan to convene the Security Council tomorrow.

KISSINGER: We have to take action. The President is blaming me, but you people are in the clear.

SISCO: That's ideal!

KISSINGER: The earlier draft for Bush is too even-handed.

SISCO: To recapitulate, after we have seen the Pak Ambassador, the Secretary will report to you. We will update the draft speech for Bush.

KISSINGER: We can say we favor political accommodation but the real job of the Security Council is to prevent military action.

SISCO: We have never had a reply either from Kosygin or Mrs Gandhi.

WILLIAMS: Are we to take economic steps with Pakistan also?

KISSINGER: Wait until I talk with the President. He hasn't addressed this problem in connection with Pakistan yet.

SISCO: If we act on the Indian side, we can say we are keeping the Pakistan situation 'under review'.

KISSINGER: It's hard to tilt toward Pakistan if we have to match every Indian step with a Pakistan step. If you wait until Monday, I can get a Presidential decision.

PACKARD: It should be easy for us to inform the banks involved to defer action inasmuch as we are so near the weekend.

KISSINGER: We need a WSAG in the morning. We need to think about our treaty obligations. I remember a letter or memo interpreting our existing treaty with a special India tilt. When I visited Pakistan in January 1962, I was briefed on a secret document or oral understanding about contingencies arising in other than the SEATO context. Perhaps it was a Presidential letter. This was a special interpretation of the March 1959, bilateral agreement.

Prepared by:
/S/ initials
James M. Noyes
Deputy Assistant Secretary for Near Eastern, African and South Asian Affairs
Approved:
(illegible signature)
For G. Warren Nutter, Assistant Secretary of Defense for International Security Affairs.

Distribution: Secdef, Depsecdef, CJCS, ASD (ISA), PDASD (ISA), DASD: NEASA & PPNSCA, Dep Dir: NSCC & PPNSCA, CSD files, R & C files, NESA.

Source: *New York Herald Tribune*, Paris edition, 6 January 1972.

(B) Account of 4 December Meeting

Covering Memorandum
THE JOINT CHIEFS OF STAFF
WASHINGTON, D.C. 20301

Secret-Sensitive
Memorandum for: Chief of Staff, U.S. Army
Chief of Staff, U.S. Air Force
Chief of Naval Operations
Commandant of the Marine Corps

SUBJECT

Washington Special Action Group meeting on Indo-Pakistan hostilities; 4 December 1971.

1. Attached for your information is a memorandum for record concerning subject meeting.

2. In View of the sensitivity of information in the N.S.C. system and the detailed nature of this memorandum, it is requested that access to it be limited to a strict need-to-know basis.

For the chairman, J.C.S.:
A. K. Knoizen
Captain, U.S. Navy
Executive assistant to the Chairman, Joint Chiefs of Staff

Report on the Meeting
Secret Sensitive
THE JOINT CHIEFS OF STAFF
WASHINGTON, D.C. 20301
5 December 1971

MEMORANDUM FOR RECORD

SUBJECT

Washington Special Action Group meeting on Indo-Pakistan hostilities; 4 December 1971.

1. The N.S.C. Washington Special Action Group met in the

Situation Room, the White House, at 1100, Saturday, 4 December, to consider the Indo-Pakistan situation. The meeting was chaired by Dr. Kissinger.

2. Attendees

A. Principals:

Dr. Henry Kissinger
Dr John Hannah, A.I.D.
Mr Richard Helms, C.I.A.
Dr G. Warren Nutter, Defense
Admiral Elmo Zumwalt, J.C.S.
Mr Christopher Van Hollen, State

B. Others:

Mr James Noyes, Defense
Mr Armistead Selden, Defense
Rear Adm. Robert Welander, O.J.C.S.
Capt. Howard Kay, O.J.C.S.
Mr Harold Saunders, N.S.C.
Col. Richard Kennedy, N.S.C.
Mr Samuel Hoskanson, N.S.C.
Mr Donald MacDonald, A.I.D.
Mr Mauric Williams, A.I.D.
Mr John Waller, C.I.A.
Mr Samuel De Palma, State
Mr Bruce Lanigen, State
Mr David Schnelder, State

3. Summary. It was decided that the U.S. would request an immediate meeting of the Security Council. The U.S. resolution would be introduced in a speech by Ambassador Bush as soon as possible. The U.S.G.–U.N. approach would be tilted toward the Paks. Economic aid for Pakistan currently in effect will not be terminated. No requirements were levied on the J.C.S.

4. Mr Helms opened the meeting by indicating that the Indians were currently engaged in a no-holds-barred attack of East Pakistan and that they had crossed the border on all sides this morning. While India had attacked eight Pak airfields there were still no indications of any ground attacks in the West. Although not decreeing a formal declaration of war, President Yahya has stated that 'the final war with India is upon us', to which Mrs Gandhi had

responded that the Pak announcement of war constituted the ultimate folly. The Indians, however, had made it a point not to declare war. The Indian attacks have hit a major P.O.L. area in Karachi resulting in a major fire which will likely be blazing for a considerable length of time, thus providing a fine target for the India air force. Mr Helms indicated that the Soviet assessment is that there is not much chance of a great power confrontation in the current crisis.

5. Dr Kissinger remarked that if the Indians have announced a full scale invasion, this fact must be reflected in our U.N. statement.

6. Mr Helms indicated that we do not know who started the current action, nor do we know why the Paks hit the four small airfields yesterday.

7. Dr Kissinger requested that by Monday the C.I.A. prepare an account of who did what to whom and when.

8. Mr De Palma suggested that if we refer to the India declaration in our discussion in the U.N., that we almost certainly will have to refer to remarks by Yahya.

9. Dr Kissinger replied that he was under specific instructions from the President, and either someone in the bureaucracy would have to prepare this statement along the lines indicated or that it would be done in the White House.

10. Mr Helms referred to the 'no holds barred' remark in the official India statement and similar remarks that were being made from the Pak side.

11. Dr Kissinger asked whether the Indians have stated anything to the effect that they were in an all-out war.

12. Mr Helms said that the terminology was 'no holds barred'.

13. Dr Kissinger asked what the Paks have said. Mr Helms said the terminology was 'final war with India'. Dr Kissinger suggested this was not an objectionable term. It did not seem outrageous to say that they (the Paks) were trying to defend themselves.

14. Dr Kissinger then asked what was happening in the U.N., to which Mr De Palma responded that the U.K., Belgium, Japan and possibly France were joining for a call for a Security Council meeting. The Japanese had detected some slight tilt in our letter requesting the meeting. The Japanese preferred a blander formulation. We have not, however, reacted to the Japanese.

15. Dr Kissinger asked to see the letter and requested that it be promulgated in announcing our move in the U.N., to which Mr De Palma responded affirmatively.

16. Dr Kissinger stated that while he had no strong view on the letter, our position must be clearly stated in the announcement.

17. Dr Kissinger stated he did not care how third parties might react, so long as Ambassador Bush understands what he should say.

18. Dr Kissinger said that whoever was putting out background information relative to the current situation is provoking Presidential wrath. The President is under the 'illusion' that he is giving instructions; not that he is merely being kept apprised of affairs as they progress. Dr Kissinger asked that this be kept in mind.

19. Mr De Palma indicated that he did not yet know whether the Security Council would be convened in the afternoon or evening (this date). However, the first statements at the meeting would likely be those by the Indians and Paks. He suggested that Ambassador Bush should be one of the first speakers immediately following the presentation by the two contesting nations. He felt that the impact of our statement would be clearer if it were made early. Dr Kissinger voiced no objections.

20. Mr De Palma asked whether we wanted to get others lined up with our resolution before we introduced it. This, however, would take time. Dr Kissinger suggested rather than follow this course, we had better submit the resolution as quickly as possible, alone if necessary. According to Dr Kissinger the only move left for us at the present time is to make clear our position relative to our greater strategy. Everyone knows how all this will come out and everyone knows that India will ultimately occupy East Pakistan. We must, therefore make clear our position, table our resolution. We want a resolution which will be introduced with a speech by Ambassador Bush. If others desire to come along with us, fine; but in any event we will table the resolution with a speech by Ambassador Bush.

21. Dr Kissinger continued that it was important that we register our position. The exercise in the U.N. is likely to be an exercise in futility, inasmuch as the Soviets can be expected to veto. The U.N.,

itself, will in all probability do little to terminate the war. He summarized the foregoing by saying that he assumed that our resolution in the U.N. will be introduced by a speech and there will be no delay. We will go along in general terms with reference to political accommodation in East Pakistan but we will certainly not imply or suggest any specifics, such as the release of Mujib.

22. Dr Kissinger asked how long the Indians could delay action in the Council. Mr De Palma said they could make long speeches or question our purpose. Mr Van Hollen said that they would draw out as long as possible which would allow them to concentrate on the situation in East Pakistan. Mr De Palma said that they could shilly-shally for three or four days which, Mr Helms stated, would be long enough for them to occupy East Pakistan. Mr De Palma stated that we could always try to force a vote. Dr Kissinger reiterated that there was no chance in getting anyting useful in the U.N.

23. Mr De Palma suggested that in all likelihood one side or the other will veto.

24. Concerning the matter of economic aid, Dr Kissinger stated that the President had directed that cutoff was to be directed at India only. He indicated, however, that he wanted to read the announcement to the President so that the latter would know exactly what he might be getting into. At this point Mr Williams asked whether some mention should be made in the statement explaining why aid for Pakistan is not being cut off. Dr Kissinger said that information would be kept for background only.

25. Mr williams said that the Department of Agriculture indicated that the price of vegetable oil was weakening in the United States; thus cutting off this P.L. 480 commodity to India could have repercussions on the domestic market. He asked, therefore, whether oil could be shipped in place of wheat. Dr Kissinger said that he will have the answer to that by the opening of business Monday.

26. Dr Kissinger then asked for a brief rundown on the military situation. Admiral Zumwalt responded that he thought the Paks could hold the line in East Pakistan for approximately one or two weeks before the logistic problems became overriding. He expected the Soviets to cement their position in India and to push

for permanent usage of the naval base at Visag. He anticipated that the Soviets' immediate short range objective would be to gain military advantages through their current relationship with India.

27. Dr Kissinger indicated that the next meeting will convene Monday morning (6 December).

/S/ H.N. Kay

H. N. Kay

Captain, U.S.N.

South Asia/M.A.P. Branch, J5

Extension 72400

Source: Ibid.

(C) Memo on 6 December Meeting

THE JOINT CHIEFS OF STAFF

WASHINGTON, D.C. 20301

6 December 1971

MEMORANDUM FOR RECORD

SUBJECT

Washington Special Action Group meeting on Indo-Pakistan hostilities; 6 December 1971.

1. The N.S.C. Washington Special Action Group met in the Situation Room, the White House, at 1100, Monday, 6 December, to consider the Indo-Pakistan situation. The meeting was chaired by Dr Kissinger.

2. Attendees

A. Principals:

Dr Henry Kissinger

Mr David Packard, Defense

Ambassador U. Alexis Johnson, State

Gen. William Westmoreland, J.C.S.

Mr Richard Helms, C.I.A.

Mr Donald MacDonald, A.I.D.

B. Others:

Mr Christoher Van Hollen, State

Mr Samuel De Palma, State

240

Mr Bruce Lanigen, State
Mr Joseph Sisco, State
Mr Armistead Selden, Defense
Mr James Noyes, Defense
Mr John Waller, C.I.A.
Mr Samuel Hoskanson, N.S.C.
Col. Richard Kennedy, N.S.C.
Mr Harold Saunders, N.S.C
Rear Adm. Robert Welander, O.J.C.S.
Capt. Howard Kay, O.J.C.S.
Mr Maurice Williams, A.I.D.

3. Summary. Discussion was devoted to the massive problems facing Bangladesh as a nation. Dr Kissinger indicated that the problem should be studied now. The subject of possible military aid to Pakistan is also to be examined, but on a very close hold basis. The matter of Indian redeployment from East to West was considered, as was the legality of the current sea 'blockade' by India.

4. Mr Helms opened the meeting by briefing the current situation. He stated that the Indians had recognized Bangladesh and the Paks had broken diplomatic ties with India. Major fighting continued in the East but India is engaged in a holding action in the West. Mr Helms felt that the Indians will attempt to force a decision in the East within the next 10 days. The Indians have almost total air superiority now in the East, where they can employ approximately a hundred of their aircraft against Pak ground forces and logistic areas. The Indians, however, have not yet broken through on the ground in East Pakistan. Major thrust of the Indian effort in East Pakistan is in the north-west corner of the province. The airfield at Dacca is all but closed The Indians are registering only minor gains in the Jessore area, but they claim to have taken Kamalpur. In the West, Indian activity is essentially limited to air attacks. The Paks appear to be on the offensive on the ground and have launched air strikes in Punjab. Overall, the Paks claim 61 Indian aircraft destroyed; the Indians claim 47 Pak planes. In naval action one Pak destroyer has been sunk by the Indians and another claimed sunked [sic]. The Indians also claim the sinking of one Pak submarine in eastern waters. Moscow is increasingly vocal in its

241

support of India and is not supporting any U.N. moves to halt the fighting. The Chinese press made its strongest attack on India this morning.

5. Dr Kissinger then asked for a military assessment, questioning how long the Paks might be able to hold out in the East. General Westmoreland responded that it might be as much as three weeks.

6. Dr Kissinger asked what is to be done with Bangladesh. Mr Helms stated that for all practical purposes it is now an independent country, recognized by India.

7. Ambassador Johnson suggested that the Pak armed forces now in East Pakistan could be held hostage. General Westmoreland reinforced this by noting there was no means of evacuating West Pak forces from the East Wing, particularly in view of Indian naval superiority.

8. Dr Kissinger stated that the next state of play will involve determining our attitude toward the state of Bangladesh.

9. Mr Williams referred to the one and a half million Urdu-speaking (Bihari) people in East Pakistan who could also be held hostage.

10. Dr Kissinger asked if there had already been some massacre of these people. Mr Williams said that he certainly thinks there will be. Dr Kissinger asked if we could do anything, to which Mr Williams stated that perhaps an international humanitarian effort could be launched on their behalf. Dr Kissinger asked whether we should be calling attention to the plight of these people now. Mr Williams said that most of these people were, in fact, centered around the rail centres; that they are urban dwellers and that some efforts on their behalf might well be started through the U.N. Dr Kissinger suggested that this be done quickly in order to prevent a bloodbath. Mr Sisco stated that while the U.N. cannot do anything on the ground at this time, public attention could be focused on this situation through the General Assembly.

11. Mr Williams referred to the 300,000 Bengalis in West Pakistan, and that they too were in some jeopardy. Mr Sisco said that this humanitarian issue could be a very attractive one for the General Assembly and that we would begin to focus on Assembly action. Mr MacDonald cited as a possible precedet the mass movement of population from North Vietnam in 1954.

12. Returning to the military picture, Mr Williams stated that he felt that the primary thrust of the Indian Army would be to interdict Chittagong and cut off any supply capability still existing for the Paks in the East. He said that he felt that the major thrust of the Indian Army in the east would be to destroy the Pak regular forces. He felt that a major job would be to restore order within the East, inasmuch as it will be faced with a massacre as great as any we have faced in the 20th century.

13. General Westmoreland suggested that the Indians would probably need three or four divisions to continue to work with the Mukti Bahini; the remainder could be pulled out to assist the Indian forces in the West.

14. Mr Sisco opined that the Indians would pull out most of their troops once the Pak forces are disarmed, inasmuch as the Indians will be working with a very friendly population; thus, they will turn the military efforts over to the Mukti Bahini as quickly as possible. He felt that the extent and timing of Indian withdrawal from East Pakistan would depend to a large degree on development in the West.

15. In response to a question, General Westmoreland stated that Indian transportation capabilities were limited from West to East, and that it would probably take at least a week to move one infantry division. It might take as much as a month to move all or most of the Indian forces from the East to the West.

16. Mr Sisco said that the long-term presence of Indian forces in Bangladesh would have to be addressed. Mr Van Hollen remarked that should be Indian Army remain more than two or three weeks after the situation in East Pakistan is wrapped up they would, in fact, become a Hindu army of occupation in the eyes of the Bengalis.

17. Mr Van Hollen raised the problem of the return of the refugee from India. Inasmuch as Bangladesh is predominantly Moslem, the return of 10 million refugees, most of whom are Hindu, would present another critical problem.

18. General Westmoreland suggested that the Indian position in the West was not unadvantageous. He briefly discussed the order of battle in West Pakistan and suggested that the Indians were in relatively good shape. He said that he expected the major Pak

243

effort to be toward Kashmir and the Punjab. The Indians, he felt, will be striking toward Hyderabad so as to cut the main L.O.C. to Karachi. He did not think that the Indians necessarily plan to drive all the way to Karachi. He also suggested that the current Indian move in that direction could very well be diversionary, in order to force the Paks to pull reserves back from the Kashmir area.

19. Mr Packard asked about the P.O.L supply situation for Pakistan. Mr Helms said that at the present time it looked very bad. The overland L.O.C.'s from Iran, for example, were very tenuous.

20. Mr Willams suggested that the reason for the Indian thrust to the south was essentially political. Inasmuch as the Indians do not want to fight on the border they will have to give ground in Kashmir. In order to ward off parliamentry criticism, Mrs Gandhi may be going for some Pak real estate in south.

21. Dr Kissinger then asked about U.N. initiatives. Mr Sisco said that we are now reviewing the situation with Ambassador Bush. Two Security Council resolutions have been vetoed by the Soviets. However, there is a ground-swell building in New York for an emergency session by the General Assembly to be convened under the provisions of the 'threat to peace' mechanism. The crisis could be moved into the Assembly through a simple majority vote.

22. Dr Kissinger and Mr Sisco agreed that any resolution introduced into the General Assembly must retain two key elements: Cease fire and withdrawal of military forces. Dr Kissinger agreed that our U.N. delegation has handled the situation extremely well to date. Mr Sisco said that although it is very likely that the crisis will be introduced in the General Assembly, we must remember that there are 136 countries represented therein, and we can expect all sorts of pressure to be generated. Mr De Palma suggested that when the resolution is introduced in the Assembly there will be a new twist, i.e.: the Indians will be no longer terribly interested in political accommodation. By that time that issue will have ceased to be a problem.

23. Mr De Palma said that a Council meeting was scheduled for 3:30 today and at that time we could try to get the Council to let go of the issue in order to transfer it to the Assembly, it being quite obvious that we are not going to get a cease-fire through the Security Council.

24. Dr Kissinger asked if we could expect the General Assembly to get the issue by the end of the day, to which Mr De Palma replied that hopefully this will be the case.

25. Dr Kissinger said that we will go with essentially the same speech in the General Assembly as was made in the Security Council, but he would like something put in about refugees and the text of our resolution.

26. Dr Kissinger also directed that henceforth we show a certain coolness to the Indians; the Indian Ambassador is not to be treated at too high a level.

27. Dr Kissinger then asked about a legal position concerning the current Indian naval 'blockade'. Mr Sisco stated that we have protested both incidents in which American ships have been involved. However, no formal proclamation apparently has been made in terms of a declaration of a war, that it is essentially still an undeclared war, with the Indians claiming power to exercise their rights of belligerency. State would, however, prepare a paper on the legal aspects of the issue. Ambassador Johnson said that so far as he was concerned the Indians had no legal position to assert a blockade.

28. Dr Kissinger asked that a draft protest be drawn up. If we considered it illegal, we will make a formal diplomatic protest Mr Sisco said that he would prepare such a protest.

29. Dr Kissinger then asked whether we have the right to authorize Jordan or Saudi Arabia to transfer military equipment to Pakistan. Mr Van Hollen stated the United States cannot permit a third country to transfer arms which we have provide them when we, ourselves, do not authorize sale direct to the ultimate recipient, such as Pakistan. As of last January we made a legislative decision not to sell to Pakistan. Mr Sisco said that the Jordanians would be weakening their own position by such a transfer and would probably be grateful if we could get them off the hook. Mr Sisco went on to say that as the Paks increasingly feel the heat we will be getting emergency requests from them.

30. Dr Kissinger said that the President may want to honor those requests. The matter has not been brought to Presidential attention but it is quite obvious that the President is not inclined to let the Paks be defeated. Mr Packard then said that we should look at

what could be done. Mr Sisco agreed but said it should be done very quietly. Dr Kissinger indicated he would like a paper by tomorrow (7 December).

31. Mr Sisco suggested that what we are really interested in are what supplies and equipment could be made available, and the modes of delivery of this equipment. He stated that from a political point of view our efforts would have to be directed at keeping the Indians from 'extinguishing' West Pakistan.

32. Dr Kissinger turned to the matter of aid and requested that henceforth letters of credit not be made irrevocable. Mr Williams stated that we have suspended general economic aid, not formally committed, to India, which reduces the level to $10 million. He suggested that what we have done for Pakistan in the same category does not become contentious inasmuch as the Indians are now mobilizing all development aid for use in the war effort, whereas remaining aid for East Pakistan is essentially earmarked for fertilizer and humanitarian relief. A case can be made technically, politically and legally that there is a difference between the aid given India and that given to Pakistan.

33. Dr Kissinger said to make sure that when talking about cutoff of aid for India to emphasize what is cut off and not on what is being continued.

34. Dr Kissinger then asked about evacuation. Mr Sisco said that the Dacca evacuation had been aborted.

35. Dr Kissinger inquired about a possible famine in East Pakistan. Mr Williams said that we will not have a massive problem at this time, but by next spring this will quite likely be the case. Dr Kissinger asked whether we will be appealed to bail out Bangladesh. Mr Williams said that the problem would not be terribly great if we could continue to funnel 140 tons of food a month through Chittagong, but at this time nothing is moving. He further suggested that Bangladesh will need all kinds of help in the future, to which Ambassador Johnson added that Bangladesh will be an 'international basket case'. Dr Kissinger said, however, it will not necessarily be our basket case. Mr Williams said there is going to be need of massive assistance and resettling of refugees, transfers of population and feeding the population. Dr Kissinger suggested that we ought to start studying this problem right now.

36. Mr Williams suggested that the Indians had consistently requested refugee aid in cash. The Indians in turn will provide the food and support for the refugees. This has provided India with a reservoir of foreign currency. Dr Kissinger also asked that this problem be looked at by tomorrow to determine whether we could provide commodities in lieu of cash. We do not want to cut off humanitarian aid. We would like to provide material rather than cash.

37. The meeting was then adjourned.

> /S/ H. N. Kay
> H. N. Kay
> Captain, U.S.N.
> South Asia/M.A.P. Branch, J5
> Extension 72400.

Source: Ibid.

(D) Memo on 8 December Meeting

Secret Sensitive
THE JOINT STAFF
THE JOINT CHIEFS OF STAFF
WASHINGTON, D.C. 20301

8 December 1971

MEMORANDUM FOR RECORD

SUBJECT

Washington Special Action Group meeting on Indo-Pakistan hostilities; 8 December 1971.

1. The N.S.C. Washington Special Action Group met in the Situation Room, the White House, at 1100, Wednesday, 8 December to consider the Indo-Pakistan situation. The meeting was chaired by Dr Kissinger.

2. Attendees

A. Principals: Dr Henry Kissinger, Mr Richard Helms, C.I.A., Gen. John Ryan, J.C.S., Mr Donald MacDonald, A.I.D., Mr David Packard, Defense, Ambassador U. Alexis Johnson, State.

247

B. Others: Mr. Maurice Williams, A.I.D., Mr John Walter, C.I.A., Col. Richard Kennedy, N.S.C., Mr Samuel Hoskanson, N.S.C., Mr Harold Saunders, N.S.C., Mr Armistead Selden, Defense, Mr James Noyes, Defense, Mr Christopher Van Hollen, State, Mr Samuel De Palma, State, Mr Bruce Lanigen, State, Mr David Schneider, State, Mr Joseph Sisco, State, Rear Adm. Robert Welander, O.J.C.S., Capt. Howard Kay, O.J.C.S.

3. Summary. Dr Kissinger suggested that India might be attempting, through calculated destruction of Pak armored and air forces, to render Pakistan impotent. He requested that the Jordanian interest in assisting Pakistan not be turned off, but rather kept in a holding pattern. He asked that Pak capabilities in Kashmir be assessed.

4. Mr Helms opened the meeting by briefing the current situation. In the East, the Indians have broken the line at Comilla. Only major river crossings prevent them from investing Dacca. The Indians are advancing rapidly throughout East Pakistan. All major Pak L.O.C.'s in the East are now vulnerable. In the West, the Paks are now claiming Poonch, inside the Indian border. However, the Paks are admitting fairly heavy casualties in the fighting. Tank battles are apparently taking place in the Sind/Rajasthan area. Mrs Gandhi has indicated that before heeding a U.N. call for cease-fire, she intends to straighten out the southern border of Azad Kashmir. It is reported that, prior to terminating present hostilities, Mrs Gandhi intends to attempt to eliminate Pakistan's armor and air force capabilities. Thus far only India and Bhutan have recognized Bangladesh. It is believed that the Soviets have held off recognition primarily so as not to rupture relations with the Paks. Soviet action on the matter of recognition, however, may be forthcoming in the near future.

5. Mr Sisco inquired how long the Paks might be expected to hold out in East Pakistan, to which Mr Helms replied 48 to 72 hours. The time to reach the ultimate climax is probably a function of the difficulties encountered in river crossings.

6. Assessing the situation in the West, General Ryan indicated that he did not see the Indians pushing too hard at this time, rather they seem content with a holding action.

7. Dr Kissinger asked how long it would take to shift Indian

248

forces from East to West. General Ryan said it might take a reasonably long time to move all the forces, but that the airborne brigade could be moved quickly, probably within a matter of five or six days.

8. Dr Kissinger inquired about refugee aid. After a discussion with Mr Williams it was determined that only a very small number of U.S. dollars earmarked for refugee relief was actually entering the Indian economy. Contrary to the sense of the last meeting, the Indians have actually lost foreign exchange in the process of caring for refugees. In any event, the entire relief effort is currently suspended in both India and Pakistan.

9. Dr Kissinger then emphasized that the President has made it clear that no further foreign exchange, PL-480 commodities, or development loans could be assigned to India without approval of the White House. Mr Williams stated there was no problem of anything sliding through.

10. Dr Kissinger inquired what the next turn of the screw might be. Mr Williams said that the only other possible option was taking a position concerning aid material currently under contract. This however would be a very messy problem inasmuch as we would be dealing with irrevocable letters of credit. Mr Williams further stated that we would have to take possession of material that was being consigned to the Indians by U.S. contractors and thus would be compelled to pay U.S. supplies, resulting in claims against the U.S.G.

11. Mr Packard said that all of this could be done, but agreed that it would be a very laborious and difficult problem. He further elaborated that all the items involved would have to be located, the United States, would have to take ownership, settle with suppliers, locate warehousing, etc. Nevertheless, if such was desired it could be done. Mr Williams said that in a very limited way this type of action had been taken against some Mid-East countries, but that it had taken years to settle the claims.

12. Dr Kissinger asked how India was handling next year's development loan program, to which Mr Williams responded that nothing was under negotiation at the present time.

13. Dr Kissinger inquired about next year's [A.I.D.] budget. Mr Williams stated that what goes into the budget did not represent

a commitment. Dr Kissinger stated that current orders are not to put anything into the budget for A.I.D. to India. It was not to be leaked that A.I.D. had put money in the budget for India, only to have the 'wicked' White House take it out.

14. Dr Kissinger suggested that the key issue if the Indians turn on West Pakistan is Azad Kashmir. If the Indians smash the Pak air force and the armored forces we would have a deliberate Indian attempt to force the disintegration of Pakistan. The elimination of the Pak armored and air forces would make the Paks defenseless. It would turn West Pakistan into a client state. The possibility elicits a number of questions. Can we allow a U.S. ally to go down completely while we participate in a blockade? Can we allow the Indians to scare us off, believing that if U.S. supplies are needed they will not be provided?

15. Mr Sisco stated that if the situation were to evolve as Dr Kissinger had indicated then, of course, there was a serious risk to the viability of West Pakistan. Mr Sisco doubted, however, that the Indians had this as their objective. He indicated that Foreign Minister Singh told Ambassador Keating that India had no intention of taking any Pak territory. Mr Sisco said it must also be kept in mind that Kashmir is really disputed territory.

16. Mr Helms then stated that earlier he had omitted mentioning that Madame Gandhi, when referring to China, expressed the hope that there would be no Chinese intervention in the West. She said that the Soviets had cautioned her that the Chinese might rattle the sword in Ladakh but that the Soviets have promised to take appropriate counter-action if this should occur. Mr Helms indicated that there was no Chinese build-up at this time but, nevertheless, even without a build-up they could 'make motions and rattle the sword'.

17. Turning then to the question of military support of Pakistan, Dr Kissinger referred to an expression of interest by King Hussein relative to the provision of F-104s to Pakistan, and asked how we could get Jordan into a holding pattern to allow the President time to consider the issue. Dr Kissinger also asked whether we should attempt to convey to the Indians and the press that a major attack on West Pakistan would be considered in a very serious light by this country.

18. Mr Packard explained that we could not authorize the Jordanians to do anything that the U.S.G. could not do. If the U.S.G. could not give the 104's to Pakistan, we could not allow Jordan to do so. If a third country had material that the U.S.G. did not have, that was one thing, but we could not allow Jordan to transfer the 104's unless we make a finding that the Paks, themselves, were eligible to purchase them from us directly.

19. Dr Kissinger suggested that if we had not cut the sale of arms to Pakistan the current problem would not exist. Mr Packard agreed.

20. Dr Kissinger suggested that perhaps we never really analysed what the real danger was when we were turning off the arms to Pakistan.

21. Mr Packard suggested that another consideration in the Jordan issue is that if Jordan delivers this equipment we would be expected to replace it. Ambassador Johnson stated we do not have any more M.A.P. left.

22. Dr Kissinger states that what we may be witnessing is a situation wherein a country equipped and supported by the Soviets may be turning half of Pakistan into an impotent state and the other half into a vassal. We must consider what other countries may be thinking of our action.

23. Mr Helms asked about our CENTO relationships with Pakistan. Ambassador Johnson stated we had no legal obligations towards Pakistan in the CENTO context. Dr Kissinger agreed but added that neither did we have legal obligations toward India in 1962 when we formulated the air defense agreement. We must consider what would be the impact of the current situation in the larger complex of world affairs.

24. Dr Kissinger said that we must look at the problem in terms of Security Council guarantees in the Mid-East and the impact on other areas. We must look at the military supply situation. One could make a case, he argued, that we have done everything two weeks too late in the current situation.

25. Mr Packard stated that perhaps the only satisfactory outcome would be for us to stand fast, with the expectation that the West Paks could hold their own.

26. Ambassador Johnson said that we must examine the possible

251

effects that additional supplies for Pakistan might have. It could be that eight F-104's might not make any difference once the real war in the West starts. They could be considered only as a token. If, in fact, we were to move in West Pakistan we would be in a new ball game.

27. Ambassador Johnson said that one possibility would be our reply to Foreign Minister Singh, in which we could acknowledge the Indian pledge that they do not have territorial designs. He also stated we must also consider the fact that the Paks may themselves be trying to take Kashmir.

28. After discussing various possible commitment to both Pakistan and India, Mr Packard stated that the overriding consideration is the practical problem of either doing something effective or doing nothing. If you don't win, don't get involved. If we were to attempt something it would have to be with a certainty that it would affect the outcome. Let's not get in if we know we are going to lose. Find some way to stay out.

29. Mr Williams suggested that we might now focus efforts for a cease-fire in West Pakistan. Ambassador Johnson stated this might, however, stop the Paks from moving into Kashmir.

30. Dr Kissinger asked for an assessment of the Pak capabilities and prospects in Kashmir. He asked C.I.A. to prepare an assessment of the international implications of Mrs Gandhi's current moves. He indicated that we should develop an initial stand on the military supply question. He reiterated that he desired to keep Hussein in a 'holding pattern' relative to the latter's expression of support for Pakistan and that he should not be turned off. The U.S.G. should indicate to Hussein that we do not consider trivial his feelings in this matter.

31. Turning to the question of the blockade, Ambassador, Johnson said that both India and Pakistan have taken blockade action, even though the Pak blockade is essentially a paper blockade. Dr Kissinger said that we should also protest to the Paks. Ambassador Johnson indicated we do not have a legal case to protest the blockade. The belligerent nations have a right to blockade when a state of war exists. We may think it unwise and we may question how it is carried out. We have, in fact, normally expressed our concern. On the other hand we have no problem in

protesting the incident of the S.S. *Buckeye State.*

32. Dr Kissinger said that we are not trying to be even-handed. There can be no doubt what the President wants. The President does not want to be even-handed. The President believes that India is the attacker. We are trying to get across the idea that India has jeopardized relations with the United States. Dr Kissinger said that we cannot afford to ease India's state of mind. 'The Lady' is cold-blooded and tough and will not turn into a Soviet satellite merely because of pique. We should not ease her mind. He invited anyone who objected to this approach to take his case to the President. Ambassador Keating, he suggested, is offering enough reassurance on his own.

33. Addressing briefly the question of communal strife in East Pakistan, Dr Kissinger asked whether anyone would be in a position to know that massacres were occurring at the time when they took place. Mr Helms indicated that we might not know immediately, but we certainly would know after a massacre occurred.

34. The meeting was adjourned at 12:10.

/S/ H. N. Kay
H. N. Kay
Captain, U.S.N.
South Asia/M.A.P. Branch, J5
Extension 72400

Source: Ibid., 15 January 1992

NOTE: Terms used in the Text

A.I.D.: Agency for International Development.

A.S.D. (I.S.A.): Assistant Secretary of Defense, International Security Affairs.

Azad Kashmir: Free Kashmir, name of the Pakistani-held parts of Kashmir.

CENTO: Central Treaty Organization.

C.I.A.: Central Intelligence Agency.

C.J.C.S.: Chairman, Joint Chiefs of Staff.

D.A.S.D., N.E.A.S.A. & P.P.N.S.C.A.: Deputy Assistant Secretary of Defense, Near Eastern, African and South Asian Affairs;

Deputy Assistant Secretary of Defense, Policy Plans and
National Security Council Affairs.

Dep. Dir., N.S.C.C. & P.P.N.S.C.A.: Deputy Director, Policy Plans
and National Security Council Affairs.

Depsecdef: Deputy Secretary of Defense.

F-104: *Starfighter* jet aircraft.

I.S.A.: International Security Affairs of Defense Department.

J.C.S.: Joint Chiefs of Staff.

L.O.C.: Line(s) of communication.

M.A.P.: Military Assistance Program.

N.E.A.: Near Eastern Affairs, Section of State Department.

N.E.S.A.: Near East and South Asia.

N.S.C.: National Security Council.

O.J.C.S.: Office of Joint Chiefs of Staff.

Paks: Pakistanis.

PL480: Public Law 480, governing surplus sent abroad as aid.

P.D.A.S.D.(I.S.A.): Principal Deputy Assistant of Defense,
International Security Affairs.

P.O.L.: Petroleum, oil, and lubricants.

P.L.: Public Law.

R & C Files: Records and Control Files.

Secdef: Secretary of Defense.

S.S. *Buckeye State:* American vessel strafed in Pakistani port.

U.S.G.: United States Government.

W.S.A.G.: Washington Special Action Group, arm of National
Security Council.

(E) Article by Mr Jack Anderson, 10 January 1972

The secret White House papers reveal some ominous similarities
between the Bay of Bengal and the Gulf of Tonkin. The Gulf of
Tonkin incident on 4 August 1964, led to America's deep
involvement in the Vietnam war.

The American public was told that North Vietnamese torpedo
boats had staged an unprovoked attack upon a United Stated
destroyer, although later evidence indicated that the attack was
actually provoked.

The risk of a similar naval incident in the Bay of Bengal caused grave apprehensions inside the State Department as a United States task force steamed toward a Soviet task force at the height of the Indian–Pakistan fighting.

On 7 December a top secret warning was flashed to Washington that 'three Soviet naval ships, a seagoing minesweeper and a tanker have begun to move northeastward into the Bay of Bengal.

'The units entered the Indian ocean from the Malacca Strait on 5 December and were located approximately 500 nautical miles east of Ceylon on 7 December.'

Urgent huddles in the White House led to a decision on 10 December to assemble in Malacca Strait a United States task force, spearheaded by the aircraft carrier *Enterprise*, the Navy's most powerful ship.

The primary purpose was to make a 'show of force' and to divert Indian planes and ships from Pakistan.

As the task force moved into position, Adml John McCain, our Pacific commander, inquired on 11 December about 'the feasibility of . . . aerial surveillance of Soviet task group located approximately 180 N M [nautical miles] south-west of Ceylon'.

Authorization was flashed back the same day 'in the event task force 74 is directed to transmit [to go through] the Strait of Malacca. At that time appropriate . . . screening-surveillance flights are authorized.'

As the American warships moved through the Strait and headed into the Bay of Bengal, even more ominous reports reached Washington from the defence intelligence agency.

'Recent indicators have been received which suggest the People's Republic of China may be planning actions, regarding the Indo-Pakistan conflict.'

A top secret message reported tersely: 'According to a reliable clandestine source, [Pakistan's] President Yahaya Khan claimed . . . today that the Chinese Ambassador in Islamabad has assured him that within 72 hours the Chinese Army will move towards the border.

'President Yahya's claim cannot be confirmed. However, recent Peking propaganda statements have become more critical of India's involvement in East Pakistan.'

From Kathmandu in the Himalayas, meanwhile, came word that both the Soviet and Indian military attachés had asked Col. Melvin Holst, the American attaché, what he knew about Chinese troop movements and United States fleet movements.

'USSR attaché Loginov', said the secret dispatch, called upon the Chinese military attaché Chao Kuang Chih in Kathmandu advising Chao that China 'should not get too serious about intervention, because USSR react, had many missiles, etc.'

Holst concluded, the dispatch added that 'both the USSR and India embassies have a growing concern that China might intervene.'

Simultaneously, the Central Intelligence Agency rushed out a top secret report that 'the Chinese have been passing weather data for locations in Tibet and along the Sino-Indian border since 8 December. The continued passing of weather data for these locations is considered unusual and may indicate some form of alert posture.'

And from New Delhi, the CIA reported: 'According to a reliable clandestine source, Prime Minister Gandhi told a leader of her Congress party that she had some indications that the Chinese intend to intervene along India's northern border. . . . Mrs Gandhi said that the Chinese action might be in the Ladakh area.'

Russia's Ambassador to India, Nikolai M. Pegov, however, promised on 13 December that the Soviets 'would open a diversionary action' against the Chinese and 'will not allow the Seventh Fleet to intervene'.

Here are the highlights of this ominous Soviet pledge, which the CIA claimed to have picked up from a 'reliable source'.

'Pegov stated that a Pakistan is trying to draw both the United States and China into the present conflict. The Soviet Union, however, does not believe that either country will intervene.

'According to Pegov, the movement of the Seventh Fleet is an effort by the U.S. to bully India, to discourage it form striking against West Pakistan, and at the same time to boost the morale of the Pakistani forces.

'Pegov noted that a Soviet fleet is now in the Indian Ocean and that the Soviet Union will not allow the Seventh Fleet to intervene.

'If China should decide to intervene in Ladakh, said Pegov, the

Soviet Union would open a diversionary action in Sinkiang.

'Pegov also commented that after Dacca is liberated and the Bangla Desh Government is installed both the United States and China will be unable to act and will change their current attitude toward the crisis.'

This is how the big powers danced precariously on the edge of the brink just before Christmas as people sang about peace on earth and good will toward men.

Source: *Daily Telegraph* (London), 10 January 1972.

Index

United Nations 97, 99, 129, 130, 131, 132, 134, 135, 136, 137, 140, 142, 156, 227, 228, 239, 242, 244, 245, 248
United Nations Security Council 59, 159, 161, 214-18, 237, 238, 244, 245
Usman, Maj 90

Wellington 23, 27 *see also* Defence Services Staff College

Westerling, Turco 20-1

Yahya Khan, Gen 31, 32, 33, 97, 101, 135, 136, 204-7, 210-11, 212-13, 214, 229, 230, 236, 237, 255
Young, Gavin 135, 144

Zaheer, Hasan 33, 138
Zaman, Lt Col 90
Zia, Maj 90